6/06

This Book

Belongs to

Mrs. Patricia Hayman

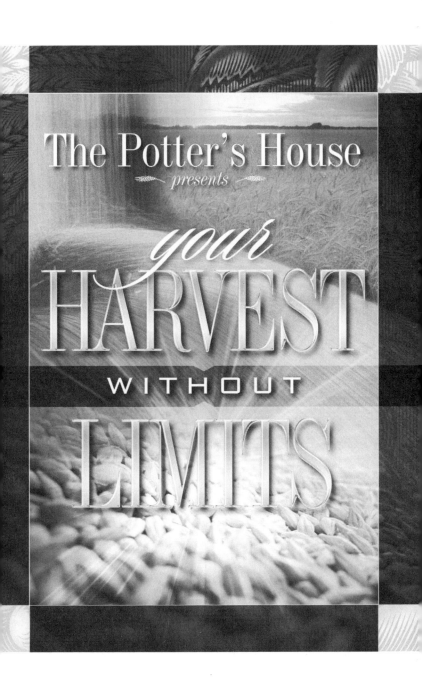

"Your Harvest Without Limits"

(ALL SCRIPTURE REFERENCES ARE IN THE KING JAMES VERSION)

TABLE OF CONTENTS

Section One – The Law of Seedtime and Harvest

Section Two – The Cycle of Reciprocity

Section Three – A Harvest on Your Praise

Section Four – The Harvests of the Wheat and Tares

INTRODUCTION

It was only a dirty Styrofoam cup on the wide ledge of an elementary school. But, contained inside that humble cup were a seed and some dirt: the basic components of a universal principle that affects all areas of life.

The principle is that of seedtime and harvest: that if you plant a seed, nurture and care for it, providing all the elements it needs to survive and thrive, it will eventually over time mature to the place that you can reap a harvest off what you planted.

It is a principle that applies not only to vegetation, but to procreation, human relationships, finance and the Word of God. Whatever we sow into a life situation or relationship, we will reap the same at harvest time.

You can learn to nurture a fruitful harvest if you develop an attitude of reciprocity, giving back to the Lord and others in gratitude for what has been received, and by maintaining patience and praise through the time of waiting for your harvest to come.

Finally, the sowing of the seed of the Word of God into your heart, and your response to that seed determines if you are a part of the current harvest of wheat or if you will face the end-of-time harvest of the tares.

A harvest without limits is waiting for you! Our prayer is that you will read this book with an open mind, let the Holy Spirit speak to your heart; and that you will learn the principles that will help you sow good seed, discover the unique harvest that God has for you, and become an aggressive reaper.

Section One: The Law of Seedtime and Harvest

"Be not deceived; God is not mocked: for whatsoever a man soweth, that shall he also reap."
(Galatians 6:7)

CHAPTER ONE:
The Agrarian Principle

Before the Industrial age, America was a land of farms and gardens; it was a land based on the agrarian principle. It was a state that valued its farms and garden plots as many families raised their own vegetables and it was typical for the families to work their plots as a family unit. Everyone, when physically able to, pitched in and tilled, planted, weeded, watered and harvested beans, collards, and other vegetables that were standard fare on the family dinner table. The food was fresh and nutritious, tasted good and helped supplement the diet for adults and children.

Sowing and Reaping
The agrarian principle carried over into school. School children were often given the assignment to plant seeds in little cups or jars to see how things germinated, developed and grew. Classroom window sills displayed the jars and cups of seeds and dirt. As the seeds sprouted and developed into full-grown plants, teachers used the growth process to teach

1

various principles about biology and life.

Through observation and first hand experience, the students became aware of the cycles of planting: burying the seed in the soil the seed sprouting into a plant, the plant developing a blossom and out of the blossom producing a fruit or vegetable which if left in the garden eventually produced a seed exactly like the original one. If you saved some of the seed through the winter you could plant them in the spring and start the cycle all over.

Those lessons left the children with a fairly good understanding of sowing and reaping; seedtime and harvest.

The Seed of the Womb

Genesis 8:22 says, *"While the earth remaineth, seedtime and harvest, and cold and heat, and summer and winter, and day and night shall not cease."* The principle of seedtime and harvest is listed in that passage with the other natural cycles of the seasons, their climate changes and the twenty-four hour cycle of night and day. This passage in Genesis makes it clear that all those cycles will continue to exist and function as laws as long as the earth is in place and spinning on its axis. As long as there is a time of planting, there will be a season of harvest.

Every facet of life that relates to us in the Kingdom of God is related to the principle of seedtime and harvest. Even as a species we procreate based on this principle. We call our process getting pregnant and having a baby. But in reality it is the same seedtime and harvest process to that of an apple tree or any other type of vegetation. The human baby is simply the harvest on the seed that is planted, gestated and developed in the womb.

When the baby comes forth out of the womb, we enjoy the harvest of that seed. The harvest of a baby creates a joy in the delivery room beyond human comprehension. When parents are expectant and prepared to receive the harvest of their seed, the birth of that baby is treated like the entrance of a movie star: the lights, camera and action of taking pictures. No one who loves their child has an ugly child. Their baby may be wrinkled, pale and scrawny, but it is beautiful to the parents, because it is their baby: the harvest of their seed.

The Farmer's Crop

Harvest is a great time, especially when you are harvesting from a positive seed in a right environment. No farmer says, "I do not feel like harvesting this crop. I am going to just let it stay out in the field and allow it to wither up and die." The farmer might get weary during the initial planting process; but when he gets ready to be on the receiving end, he is up in the pre-dawn, early hours of the morning, out in the field, reaping the harvest that he has expectantly waited for.

For the farmer, and for us, the harvest is the blessing. The farmer sows his seed for the express intent that he will bring forth a fruitful harvest. When he plants his corn, wheat or soybeans into the ground it is like taking a dividend on the former crop in the hopes that he will produce another crop.

"Your Harvest Without Limits"

The seed he plants is valuable because he could have eaten it, but he knows that there is greater value in sowing a small portion of the last crop towards an increase at the next harvest.

No farmer picks all of his produce and takes it to market without reserving some of his seeds for the next year. If he fails to save seed for the upcoming year, he in essence aborts the future. The reality is that the farmer's future harvest is in the seed. Your future harvest is in your seed. If you eat up all your seed you will not have anything to sow for next year. If you are going to perpetuate the crop in your life into another year, save some of the harvest to put aside to sow into next year's crop.

The Seed of the Tithe

The principle of seedtime and harvest is why the Bible presents us the concept of tithing. Similar to the farmer, you take some of your seed—ten percent of what you have earned—and set it aside so that you will have seed to sow for a future harvest. People who understand this principle are forward thinking people, always sowing into their future. They understand that the sacrifice of the tithe, literally a few handfuls of seed, will produce a rich harvest and that the sacrifice is meager when compared to what is eventually reaped.

If you are not forward thinking a spirit of unbelief can set in your heart and say: "I am going to hold on to what I have." The essence of that statement communicates that you do not believe that God is going to bless you beyond what you

4

currently have, so you have to hoard what you have, and protect it because it may be the last you will ever see. How foolish if the farmer would plant his crop, reap the harvest and eat up all that he reaps because he does not believe that he is ever going to see another harvest.

When we give to the work of the gospel by sowing financial seeds into the kingdom we eventually reap a harvest of our giving. And, the wonderful truth is that the harvest is always greater than what is sown. If the farmer sets aside some seed and sows that seed on good ground, he will reap an increase of some thirty, some sixty, some one-hundred-fold return off of his investment (Mark 4:8).

You Reap What You Sow

"Be not deceived; God is not mocked: for whatsoever a man soweth, that shall he also reap. For he that soweth to his flesh shall of the flesh reap corruption; but he that soweth to the Spirit shall of the Spirit reap life everlasting. And let us not be weary in well doing: for in due season we shall reap, if we faint not." (Galatians 6:7-9)

An understanding of the principle of the harvest can have an affect on every area of your life: your finances, relationships, health and spiritual well-being. Simply stated, if you want to reap something, you must sow the same. If you want to harvest friends, you must sow friendship. If you do not show yourself friendly, you cannot harvest friends. If you want to reap loyalty, you must be loyal. Regardless of the type of seed that you plant in the field of your life, you will reap whatever you sow.

"Your Harvest Without Limits"

The Galatians six passage says, "*Be not deceived; God is not mocked...*" (6:7). That 'God is not mocked' statement communicates that God is very committed to make sure the next part of the verse happens: "*...whatsoever a man soweth, that shall he also reap*" (6:7). Every farmer knows that you cannot sow tomatoes and reap onions. If you do not like collards, do not plant collards, because if you do you will reap a harvest of collards.

Do not deceive yourself because God is certainly not mocked; the principle is a truism that you cannot sow one thing and reap something else. As it is in the farmer's field, so too is it in our life in the Kingdom of God. When you sow to the spirit–in prayer, reading the Word, fellowship with other believers, obeying God, loving your neighbor–you will reap everlasting life; when you sow to the flesh—lying, cheating, sensuality, anger, evil speech and thoughts—of the flesh you will reap corruption.

I Do Not Like My Harvest!

Your life is always harvesting something. Even when the farmer decides not to plant in a field for a season, he still gets a harvest of a lot of weeds and a few isolated small patches of corn, soybeans or wheat, where stray seeds planted months before that lay dormant through the last planting cycle, finally decide to germinate and sprout. The farmer knows that he alone determines what the harvest in his fields will be. He can change the fruit of his harvest by the type of seed that he sows in the next planting cycle.

If you do not like what is being harvested in your life then all you have to do is change what you are sowing; you have the power to change the harvest in your life! Unfortunately, you have already sowed a lot of mixed seeds in your life. When you make up your mind that you are going to change what you are sowing, you will need to make a long-term commitment. It will not work to decide to change your sowing and only wait a couple of days to see if the new sowing works. Like the farmer, you have some unborn seeds that are in the ground from things that you did in the past that are already festering and developing.

But, if you want to break the cycle so you do not spend the next ten years harvesting corrupt fruit in your life, just break the cycle by planting right things and have patience. The Bible says, *"...ye have need of patience, that, after ye have done the will of God, ye might receive the promise"* (Hebrews 10:36). If you want to break the harvest cycle in your life, change what you are sowing; then have the patience to wait for the new things you are sowing to germinate and develop in your life, and you shall bring forth a fresh harvest, pressed down, shaken together and running over.

"Every facet of life is related to the principle of seedtime and harvest. Your future harvest is in your seed."

CHAPTER TWO:

Do You Have What it Takes to be a Reaper?

Today, it seems that many preachers and teachers in churches and on television are teaching about sowing, but rarely do we hear a message on the believer's role as a reaper. In the next few sections, we will discuss this principle called reaping...

The Omitted Skill

The term reaping is synonymous to harvest time: the time when you bring in what you have sown. The act of reaping literally refers to your responsibility to bring in the harvest.

Not only is it modern day preachers and teachers, but also past generations of preachers who neglected to tell us that beyond sowing there is a part that the believer has to play in the reaping of their harvest. It's possible they omitted the reaping part of the message because they were raising an offering. The sowing message is a very effective message for an evangelist who drives into town, preaches about sowing and leaves town once the closing prayer is finished.

On the contrary, it is a very different scenario for a pastor who lives with the people while they sowed and is still with the people while they are scratching their heads trying to figure out why they did not reap. A preacher can teach a lot of different messages when they are on their way out the back door to catch their jet; but if you have to stay with the people, you better make sure your message makes some sense.

Aggressive Reaping

Since the Bible tells us in Genesis 8:22 that as long as the earth is in place, seedtime and harvest will always exist, we understand that it is a principle that will work for anybody of any ethnic persuasion, economic status or educational level. And as a timeless principle, it will work for this generation and our children's generation the same as it did for grandpa; the principle will work if you work it. The problem that most people experience is that they do not understand that the reaping phase of the equation is just as aggressive as sowing.

For the past couple decades, preachers have told us that sowing is an action, but they failed to teach us that reaping is also an action. We have a whole generation that we taught to sow. And, many believers have taken that teaching, mixed it with faith and they actively sow into their marriages, jobs, families, and then go home, curl up on the sofa with a good book, and wait on the harvest. But the harvest is not going to drive up to your house, walk the path to the front door, ring your doorbell and come into your house. The harvest is not going to meet you in your living room. The harvest is not magic!

Ask any farmer if after he sowed a field of wheat, if he then went back in the house, sat down in his easy chair and waited until the harvest came into his house. As silly as that sounds, we have all kinds of believers who have sowed financially, spiritually, and with their time and are sitting around their homes and saying that they are waiting on the Lord to drop by. If that is you, my word for you is "He is not coming!" He is not coming in to make you reap any more than He came in and made you sow.

For some individuals from Pentecostal and Charismatic traditions, we have erroneously thought that reaping is an anointing. We believe that the anointing of the Holy Spirit is going to come upon us and make us receive – it is not going to happen. *"Be not deceived; God is not mocked: for whatsoever A MAN soweth, that shall HE also reap"* (Galatians 6:7). According to that passage the same man doing the sowing is the same one doing the reaping.

God is not going to reap your harvest and bring it into your house for you. If you fail to see your role in reaping your harvest, you can spend years waiting on something to happen that could have happened a long time before. The reason that it did not happen is that even though you faithfully sowed your seed, you weren't aggressive after you sowed and you did not demand a return on what you sowed.

Faint Not!

The key to a successful harvest is surviving the sowing stage and making it to the reaping stage and not fainting. The

"Your Harvest Without Limits"

Word says, *"...let us not be weary in well doing: for in due season we shall reap, if we faint not"* (Galatians 6:9). The prerequisite to success is 'if you faint not.' And the more you feel like fainting, the more it is a sign that you are closer to your reaping. For those of you who are tired, weary and even delirious; if you are feeling like everything is spinning in your life; if you feel like fainting, it is only a sign that you are close to your harvest, and you shall reap in due season if you faint not.

If you did not faint way back during the difficult early years of your life, you are not going to faint now. The devil should not even try to think he is going to trick you into fainting now; after all these years, and all the suffering, agonies and pain. You are about to come into your season and reap a harvest, and he thinks you're going to get light-headed now and give up on your dream. The Bible promises that *"...he which hath begun a good work in you will perform it until the day of Jesus Christ"* (Philippians 1:6). With that promise in hand, you would be foolish to faint now.

Have you gone through a stage in life where you were just about to faint. You got light-headed and everything in your life was spinning. That is how it feels when you are about to faint: you have lost control of everything, everything is spinning. You begin to feel that you do not care anymore: you get tired, you have been through too much. Yet when you begin to think of what you've been through and come to your senses, you say, "Wait a minute. I am dizzy but I cannot faint now. I have been through too much stuff to lie down and let the devil have me now."

Encourage yourself by saying, "I am not going to faint right now. I believe that I am coming into my season to be blessed, my moment of destiny and my season to prosper. I have been through hell, sowing and reaping; I have endured suffering and hardship. I have done without and had nobody to talk to or lean on. If I should have died, I should have died way back then. But I have come this far and I absolutely refuse to endure the hell of sowing and not be ready for the reward of blessing."

Fight and Reap

If you are in a fight, keep on reaping while you fight; fight with one hand and reap with the other. You only have a certain, limited season to reap, and the reason you have warfare is that the devil is trying to distract you and make you miss your season. Do not back off, give up or give in to his taunting. Determine to stand firm, slap him with one hand while you pluck the fruit of your harvest with the other. It is your time and season, so go for it.

The Bible says, "...*be not weary in well doing*" (2 Thessalonians 3:13); it did not say anything about well-waiting. You cannot afford to stop doing because reaping is about doing. "*Even so faith, if it hath not works, is dead, being alone*" (James 2:17). Why should pastors lay hands on someone and pray for a harvest when the person just walked away from the harvest that God already gave them. That job or circumstance that you currently find yourself in may not be your ultimate harvest, but if you are faithful over the few things, God will make you ruler over much (Matthew 25:23).

"Regardless of the type of seed you plant in the field of your life, you will reap whatever you sow."

CHAPTER THREE:

A Time to Sow and a Time to Reap

It Does Not Work for Me

An evangelist was speaking at a church on the West Coast and a lady from the church choir came out of the choir stand and approached him. Her face looked a bit confused and she was wringing her hands when she said, "Sir, I do not know what to do. I pay my tithes, sow seeds and I am still broke. I am about to be evicted from my home, my checks are bouncing all over the place, I am at the end of my rope and I do not know what in the world to do!"

Just as the man opened his mouth to say something, she cut him off and continued her monologue: "I quit my job because I want to do something for the Lord and I do not understand why He is not meeting my needs." The preacher replied, "He was! Until you quit your job He was meeting your needs." She said, "He is the one that told me to quit." He said, "He did not!" She replied, "He said He was going to use me in a powerful way." The minister said, "Was going to and 'is' are two different things."

"Your Harvest Without Limits"

There is a timing associated with every vision. When God gives you a vision for your harvest it is for a certain time and season. Sometimes you may experience hardships in your life because you rushed into something that was for a due season in your life that has not come to pass yet. Then when you get into trouble, you act like the Word does not work. The imbalance here is that you cannot just take one Scripture and make it work out of context. You cannot decide you are going to have your harvest time when you haven't sowed or when you have all your credit cards maxed out because of unnecessary shopping binges.

The Middle Part

The Bible says to, "*train up a child in the way he should go: and when he is old, he will not depart from it*" (Proverbs 22:6). That passage talks about the child and when the child is old, but it does not say anything about the middle part. The truth is that there is a delay factor between seedtime and harvest. You do the sowing into your children in their youth, but you may not reap the fruit of that sowing when you think you should. Even so, it is a biblical principal that if you sowed into your child, sooner or later what you put into them is going to come up out of the chaos of the middle period of their life.

You have a right to expect a harvest where you made an investment. But, where you have not invested the time or effort into a situation or relationship, you have no right to expect anything. It is amazing to see the people who try to harvest and cash in on a relationship where they have not made a real investment. People do not mind asking for anything and then get mad when they are told, "no" – they do not understand seedtime and harvest.

Weed Your Garden

Do not expect to reap anything that is not yours. But if you sowed something, expect to receive the return on that which is sowed. Go after that which is sowed, and that is what you will reap. If you see something sprouting up that is contradictory to what you sowed, do not receive it. If it is something that you do not deserve, don't let anyone force it on you. If you deserve it, but do not like it, repent from it, plead the blood over it, break the curse, and still take it back.

Refuse to take a whipping you did not deserve and go home feeling sorry for yourself because someone put something on you that was not for you in the first place. Stop allowing folks to make you reap things that you did not sow by putting you on a guilt trip and making you take home something that you did not deserve. You have got to break that curse, pull up those weeds and say, "This is not my harvest, these are weeds in my garden and I am going to pull them up."

It is time to weed your garden. All that stuff that you did not sow, pull it up. Everything the enemy is trying to do to you, pull it up. If you do not, it will attempt to steal the life and nutrition that should be directed toward your harvest. Tell the devil that this is not your harvest and you are not going to take it.

17

"Your Harvest Without Limits"

Don't you tire of weak Christians who just sit back and let life beat them up? You have been through too much and you've seen too much to fool around and miss your harvest. You need to stop crying; dry your tears and aggressively go after what the Bible says you have a right to.

Rotten Figs on the Vine

Did you know that your harvest can show up, but if no one taught you how to reap your harvest, you can miss it and the figs will rot on the vine? The gardener knows that there is a window of opportunity for him to harvest his vegetables. If he is too eager and reaps before the appointed time, the tomatoes will be green and hard, the carrots only bite-size and the other vegetables pale or infantile in their development. And if he waits until the harvest season is past, the produce, the fruit of his sowing, will shrivel up and die on the vine. There is a time to sow and a time to reap.

Unfortunately, too many people have spent large segments of their lives looking over the fence at their neighbor's harvest. They drool over the ripe produce that is the fruit of the neighbor's sowing, while their own harvest is rotting. Until you get to the point where you clearly see your own harvest you will spend your precious time coveting what others have and get bitter when they refuse to share their harvest with you. You do not need to see someone else's harvest; you need to focus your attention on the crop that is in your yard and learn to reap it before it rots.

"If you did not faint during the difficult early years of your life, you are not going to faint now."

CHAPTER FOUR:

Show Me My Harvest

THAT Shall He Also Reap!

"Be not deceived; God is not mocked..." is a principle that works in all areas of life. *"...whatsoever a man soweth, THAT shall he also reap"* (Galatians 6:7). Your fervent, daily prayer needs to be: "Lord, let me see my THAT. Stop letting me try to reap things that I have no rights over. Stop me from being confused about what I should be reaping." Stop me from trying to cash in on other people's gifts. You cannot reap what belongs to others; you have to reap what is yours.

You need to see your 'that' because your 'that' is distinctive from anybody else's 'that.' If it is someone else's 'that,' you cannot have it. You do not have to stay up all night trying to fight to defend what is yours. If it is yours it will not work for someone else; you cannot effectively fight in another's armor, and you will not find success if you try to use their stuff. If it is for someone else, you cannot have it and it would not work for you even if you tried.

One of the first things God told Israel when they got out in the wilderness was that while they were walking through their desert they should not covet their neighbor's ox, ass, or cattle. God did not want to get them out there and have them looking over their shoulder in another's field wishing they had their neighbor's possessions. This is what we call a covetous spirit. Anyone who is covetous has a negative faith because they do not believe that God is going to give them their own. But when you believe that God has got something for you, you do not mind me being blessed because you know that you are next in line.

When you have found your 'that,' you do not have to be stressed, intimidated, jealous or worried about anything. You do not have to be good at everything, but you must be good at something.

Pray for God to help you to find your 'that.' You have a legal right to reap the 'that' that you sowed. You can bring out of yourself what God put in you; you cannot bring out of yourself anything that is not in you, but for God's sake birth everything of the creative potential that God placed down inside you. Do not abort your harvest.

The Abundance of the Harvest

For some of you the harvest that you are shouting about is nothing compared to the future harvest that you are going to get. But because you are currently faithful over little, get ready for much because much is coming your way. The Bible says that He would "*pour you out a blessing, that there shall not be room enough to receive it*" (Malachi 3:10). You do not need fifty blessings; you just need one blessing because God said that He would bring so much out of that one blessing that it would flow out over the edges of your life because you won't have room to contain it.

If you can successfully find your 'that,' it may be the thing that will bless you for the next twenty or thirty years. The Old Testament prophet Elijah survived on the nourishment of one meal for forty days. When God is the one who fills you, you do not get hungry fast. You can run a long time off one blessing if you learn how to reap it.

People get jealous of you and cop an attitude about you when you learn how to reap because they are sitting there passively waiting for their harvest to come in and you are actively reaping yours. But when you know it is your due season and it is reaping time, you have to aggressively pursue your 'that.' For too long preachers have taught the sowing half of the principle but not the second half; the problem is that if you teach people how to sow and not to reap they soon run out. But if you keep teaching your sowers to reap, they keep sowing and reaping and go from level to level.

Sow According to Your Faith

When you reap something, do not spend everything from your harvest; sow something. And do not ever stop your sowing based on your friends. Their faith may only be in the first grade while you may already be in college. You have got to operate on the level of your faith because the Bible says, "...*according to your faith be it unto you*" (Matthew 9:29). If you are in college, you cannot run with people in the first grade because they will drag you back into 'stinking thinking' and discourage you from operating on your level.

People will attempt to discourage you from moving in your level of faith because for them it looks like too much for you to have. But you are not the one to tell me what is too much for God to do for me. For example, do not let someone else tell you what is too much to give to your spouse. You can say what is too much to give to your spouse because that is your mate, but give whatever you want to. Others were not present when you went through what you went through. You may feel strongly about your mate because of your history together, think about how much more God thinks about His people.

You do not know how much God wants to bless another person; you do not know what they've been through together while sowing in tears. The Bible says, "*They that sow in tears shall reap in joy. He that goeth forth and weepeth, bearing precious seed, shall doubtless come again with rejoicing, bringing his sheaves with him*" (Psalm 126:5-6). For those of you that have sown in tears, hell and high water, would it not be foolish to survive the sowing stage and faint at the reaping stage? If you had enough strength in the sowing stage, you need to refuse to get down to the reaping stage and collapse on the floor and let somebody else have your stuff.

Get Your Stuff

Are you tough enough to be a reaper? Reaping is controversial; no one bothers you when you are sowing; it is when you start reaping, when you finally get your child through college, that people get an attitude. Nobody was bothering you when you were working an extra part-time job to get your child into college; they did not have an attitude when you were picking your child up from the delinquent center trying to breathe the breath of life into them. But when you start getting it together, and see success break out in your family then they get an attitude.

No one was trying to take your husband when he was still Mr. Slick Willie and Dirty Danny. But now that you have invested years in your man, seen him come to the Lord, get his act cleaned up, and experienced the restoration of all that was broken in your relationship now she wants to steal your husband. The devil is a liar! You sowed too much into that relationship, and no one else has the right to reap the fruit of your sowing.

Tell her to back off your husband and go find herself a single man that she can invest in with the hope for a future harvest she can call her own.

The Best is Yet to Come

Believe in harvest. See the potential for a harvest when other people only see hell. Always believe that God is going to bless you. Believe it when the lights are out and when the gas is off. You have to look beyond the difficulties in your current situation to see the coming harvest. God is going to bring you into your season.

Church choirs often sing a favorite song titled, 'The Best is yet to Come.' And amazingly, people going through the worst times in their life get happy and do not even understand why they are getting happy. But the Holy Spirit is the one who knows that the best is yet to come, and God is trying to strengthen them to go through their difficulties. God would not have taken any of us through all that we experience if He did not have something better for us up ahead. If God wanted to kill you, He could have done it in the sowing stage. Why get to the reaping stage and give up now?

When the Holy Spirit gives you what we call a vision, it is actually a glimpse of the things that God has in store for you. The reason the Holy Spirit can only give a partial glimpse to you is that what God has in store for you is in the Spirit. "*But as it is written, Eye hath not seen, nor ear heard, neither have entered into the heart of man, the things which God hath prepared for them that love him. But God hath revealed them unto us by his Spirit…*" (I Corinthians 2:9-10).

So God will show you something that is way far away and you will catch a glimpse of it. And if you are truly a visionary, a vision will not make any sense to your current situation or understanding. If your situation looks like your vision, then you are not there yet. Your vision should be so far beyond your situation that it takes faith to believe that somebody in your current state of affairs could ever get from here to that. Be assured that once you have been tested, you too shall come forth as pure gold!

> *"You have to look beyond the difficulties in your current situation to see the coming harvest. The best is yet to come."*

24

Chapter Five:

Pursue Your Harvest

"And Naomi had a kinsman of her husband's, a mighty man of wealth, of the family of Elimelech; and his name was Boaz. And Ruth the Moabitess said unto Naomi, Let me now go to the field, and glean ears of corn after him in whose sight I shall find grace. And she said unto her, Go, my daughter. And she went, and came, and gleaned in the field after the reapers: and her hap was to light on a part of the field belonging unto Boaz, who was of the kindred of Elimelech. And behold, Boaz came from Bethlehem, and said unto the reapers, The LORD be with you. And they answered him, The LORD bless thee."
(Ruth 2:1-4)

Give Me a Corner to Glean

The young girl, Ruth followed the older Naomi into what must have been a utopia: where there was a rich harvest and people were getting blessed and reaping all around. And when she entered into that scene, she did not come in a competitive spirit, trying to teach everyone; she simply positioned herself over in the corner watching. Ruth told Naomi, "I am just here; I do not know what to do. I think I want to glean over in the corner of Boaz's field." Naomi told her to go.

What Naomi did is all you can really do for others: point people in the right direction. Naomi did not go over in the field and harvest for Ruth. The truth is that no one can go to work for you, solve all your problems nor pay all your bills. You can, however, be pointed in the right direction. After Naomi told her to go, it was Ruth that had the task of going. And that she did: Ruth went over in the corner of Boaz's field waiting to catch whatever she could.

Boaz eventually came out and saw Ruth in the field. He said to the reapers, "Let us start a cycle for seedtime and harvest. Do not pick up everything that you can. Leave a handful of wheat behind on purpose." In making that command of the reapers, Boaz understood that their bags were not going to be as full as they would have been. But when you know that another generation is coming behind you, leave some on purpose so that they can get a taste of gleaning.

A Charity Blessing

When Boaz instructed the reapers to leave some wheat behind on purpose, it was what we could call a 'charity blessing.' A charity blessing is a temporary blessing meant to sustain you while you are in the school of faith. But once you graduate from this test in faith's school, it is time to move on to the next grade. God never meant for you to spend the rest of your life waiting for someone to get through with a dress so you can wear it as a hand-me-down. He is just trying to get you though a temporary period of your life to prepare you so that you can be more productive.

Since the season is temporary you should know that the charity blessing will some day stop. And, anytime someone has been leaving you little handfuls of blessings and they stop doing it, do not get angry because they stop. When the charity ceases it means that you are ready to move up to the next level. So here we have Ruth gleaning in the fields behind the reapers, picking up the handfuls of blessing that they leave for her. If you are going to get behind somebody, be like Ruth and please get behind a reaper. How are you going to follow somebody that is not going anywhere?

Will You Please Move Ahead?

Never follow a leader who does not know anything, have anything or think anything. If you are a leader that means that you have to be in front and there is nothing worse than following someone who will not move forward. People are always complaining about the traffic. But, the traffic is not really a problem. Traffic only becomes a problem when you are stuck behind somebody who will not move. If you are going to be behind somebody, get behind a reaper.

It is a sad situation for the women who marry men who will not move. Sometimes the woman is more creative and aggressive than the man. And a dilemma is created in that he is lazy and trifling, yet the Bible says for her to be a helpmeet. The woman is put in the awkward position of trying to be a helpmeet for someone who will not move. How can you help somebody that will not move? You want to be a helpmeet for somebody that has a vision, goal and a purpose.

You do not even want to sit behind or live beside somebody who will not move. And please do not listen to or serve a preacher who will not move. It is very difficult, if you have any sense at all, to get behind a reaper and not learn something about reaping. It is as simple as following them. People who are jealous curse themselves because they talk about people they should be following. The same God that blessed the reaper will bless you too.

The Walking, Talking Harvest

Ruth got behind the reapers and they started to leave some handfuls of grain on purpose. And Ruth began to glean behind them for a season. After awhile Ruth returned to Naomi and said, "I have been gleaning behind the reapers, but that is not really my harvest. My harvest is Boaz and not his field." That old woman Naomi, who was married once but never married again knew how to tell Ruth how to bring in her harvest. Boaz was her harvest; the harvest existed before she reaped it, but sitting back and waiting on Boaz was not going to cut it.

Because you have to be a reaper, you have to be a receiver. If you are going to believe God for some real estate, you better get out of your house and start looking at some property and talking to some banks about doing some deals. A reaper takes action. Naomi told Ruth that to reap her Boaz she needed to wash her face, change her clothes, put some oil on her face and go in his room in the evening and lay down at the foot of his bed and say, "cover me with your skirts."

My point is that Boaz was a walking, talking harvest. He was a rich and successful man. He did not come to her; she came to him. The harvest of wheat does not come to the farmer; the farmer goes to the wheat. The harvest does not come to the reaper; the reaper goes to the harvest. Ruth had to actively reap from the field, and actively pursue her true harvest: Boaz.

The Violent Take it by Force

Before you go to the harvest, you have to make sure it is yours. Do not try to reap somebody else's harvest; that is theft. That is why God told Joshua and Israel when they came to Jericho, "*I have given you the land to possess it*" (Numbers 33:53). Joshua was able to successfully fight the Canaanites because he knew this was Israel's land. You have got to find your 'that,' When you find your 'that,' do not let anyone drive you away from it. Aggressively pursue something that God says is yours.

Ruth got down in the corner in Boaz's room. She said to him, "Cover me with your skirts." Here we see the reaper coming to the harvest. The question for you is, "do you have what it takes to be a reaper?" For some of you reading this book, your figs are rotting on the vine and your fruit is withering on the tree. Your harvest keeps coming in and yet you keep praying for something that God has already done. And all you have to do is be aggressive enough and go after the thing that God has given you.

"Your Harvest Without Limits"

For those of you who are weeping and suffering the
word is that *"...the kingdom of heaven suffereth violence,
and the violent take it by force..."* (Matthew 11:12). It is
imperative to raise up a radical generation that stops feeling
sorry for themselves. So many leaders in many communities
have done more damage than good by misrepresenting their
followers to the world: telling them they are poor, destitute
and desperate, and if folks do not help them they will never
have anything.

You do not need anybody pumping your head with the "you
cannot get up, do nothing, somebody's got to feel sorry for
me" type message. What you need is for others to step out of
the way and give you a chance. You are well, able, strong,
gifted, and talented. And you can still get your stuff. Other
people do not have to feel sorry for you and do not have to
help you. You have got all the capacity that the greatest of
men have ever had. And if you are given half a chance, you
will harvest your own field.

Get Up and Fight

Refuse to spend the next twenty years of your life waiting on
everybody to like you or give you permission to get what they
have. You owe it to yourself to understand who you are as a
person and step up to the forefront. It is your responsibility
to rebuke the darkness and teach your children that they are
somebody; that they can do whatever God says they can do
and have whatever God says they can have.

Do not feel at risk. You are not at risk. You were never at
risk, no more than anybody else. You are not underprivileged.

30

You have your right mind; you are gifted, blessed, anointed and bad. You are fine. You are strong and have a living Savior that loves you the same as He loves everyone else. Do not feel sorry for yourself. You are not a second class anything. In truth, you can do anything you put your mind to: you can run any company, be a soldier in the army or a construction worker.

There was a time when no one who spoke in tongues had a decent church with pews and stained glass windows. Most churches met in storefronts, shanties and tent meetings and led worship with raggedy, second-hand drums, worn out tambourines and beating on the back of coffee cans to keep the beat. But, take a few minutes to visit churches and look at where Christians worship now. It does not matter where you start, it matters how you finish. You have what it takes to get up and fight because God is for you.

The Tools for the Harvest

There are tools that are necessary for reaping. Once you identify your harvest and your 'that,' then you are going to need some tools to bring in your 'that.' Nobody goes to reap empty handed. You need something to work with. Shape your prayer life into something that makes sense to God. Rise from a position of laying down on the altar weeping about your past, crying about the boss that fired you, the person that did not give you a chance, the spouse that left and the kitten that will not come back home and all the other pitiful dead stuff that you cannot change.

"Your Harvest Without Limits"

Turn your faith into something that is futuristic, powerful and relevant to your life. It is time to get into shape, to call your house to order. There is no such thing as underprivileged to a child of God. You do not need more money, you need more God. It's better to have God than to have money because there are plenty of rich people that have money but no sense. If God is on your side, you can get the money.

There's a man working on a business deal right now. The Chief Operating Officer of his company said that he does not have what it takes to get the deal done. When told that, something leaped up inside of him and he said, "Oh, good!" When you tell him he does not have enough, he gets excited because it is a sure sign that he is going to get it.

"A reaper takes action. The harvest does not come to the reaper; the reaper goes to the harvest."

Section Two – The Cycle of Reciprocity

"Give, and it shall be given unto you; good measure, pressed down, and shaken together, and running over, shall men give into your bosom..."
(Luke 6:38)

CHAPTER SIX:

Reciprocity

The Law of Reciprocity

Reciprocity is where we get the word reciprocate. To reciprocate is to give back; it is to return something to someone who has given to you and thus create a cycle of giving. When something comes at you, you send something back toward it. If somebody is nice to you, you respond with niceness. Reciprocity is if you do something kind for me, I do something kind back to you. I reciprocated that kindness back to you.

Reciprocity is much deeper than what you learned from Miss Manners in the first grade. It is a Kingdom principle that affects and controls the natural elements and supernatural worlds alike. For example, the reason that we continually have rain that falls out of the heavens is that yesterday's rainfall dehydrated and returned back to the sky in reciprocity, feeding the ongoing cycle. When fresh rainfall is needed, we have it again because of the law of reciprocity.

"Your Harvest Without Limits"

Drought and death occur any time the law of reciprocity is broken. If you annually plant a garden but never fertilize that garden, after a few seasons the soil will be depleted of necessary nutrients. Once it is depleted of that which is life giving, the next time you plant, nothing will grow because you broke the law of reciprocity. During the autumn months, the reason your tree's leaves turn brown, wither, fall to the ground, turn into mulch and re-enter the soil is that God replenishes the soil through the principle of reciprocity. If you ever break that principle of reciprocity your soil will become acidic and dry and fail to be potent enough to reproduce again.

Don't Break the Cycle

The reason you have been blessed and continue to be blessed in your life is due to the principle of Reciprocity. Luke clearly explains the principle when He says, "*Give, and it shall be given unto you; good measure, pressed down, and shaken together, and running over, shall men give into your bosom...*" (Luke 6:38). If you ever break the cycle and stop giving you will stop the fertility of your life, and eventually, over time, you will wither.

Whenever anyone says that they break the law all the time and are still blessed, that is just as silly as Adam, who was a partaker of the forbidden fruit, saying, "Look God, I ate the fruit and I did not die." Ask Adam what happened the day he ate the forbidden fruit. While he did not physically die that day, he died spiritually. And, slowly, over time, there was an outward sign in his body of an inward decay.

The Lord said that "*the day that thou eatest thereof thou shalt surely die,*" (Genesis 2:17) and Adam died spiritually the moment he disobeyed God. It might have taken some time for his outer life to reveal what had happened in his inner life, but the time came where physical death followed what had started on the inside. The principle is the same for us: when we break God's law it often does not immediately show outwardly that we disobeyed, but it sets in motion a curse that will work out in our life for years to come.

A Childish Attitude

There is a childishness that leads people to believe that giving is all about them and what they can get out of it. It is a childishness that is completely focused on what a person needs. When this childish attitude is left unchallenged and undeveloped it will eventually destroy anything it touches. Friendships and working relationships alike will suffer because friends and co-workers will tire of feeling manipulated by the one who is self-focused.

This childish attitude is the primary reason for divorce in any marriage. People who get married because they need something soon get divorced because they did not get it. Anytime you enter into a relationship based on what you need, you are bound to be disappointed. No man or woman is Mr. or Miss Perfect, and thus will not be able to meet your every need precisely when you need it. They will bring to the marriage relationship certain facets that will be a great blessing to you, but they are not God, and therefore cannot meet your every need.

A marriage only works when you enter into it with the attitude of what you can give. When you focus on giving instead of being primarily concerned about meeting your needs, you are on the right track and resist any possibility of disappointment.

35

"Your Harvest Without Limits"

When your focus is on somebody else and you take no thought to what you need, as you give to them, you will reap whatsoever you sow.

The Selfishness of Sin

Selfishness is at the root of all sin regardless of what the sin consists of. For example, there is a vast difference between lust and love. Even though both love and lust often manifest themselves through similar avenues and consummate themselves through the same act, their root is totally different. The root of lust revolves around what I can get out of a situation or person; love is about what I can give. Lust takes and is selfish; love gives.

As many have done before, you might mistake lust and think it is love. For the confused, instead of saying, "I am in love with you" we ought to change it to, "I am in lust with you." The nature of lust is that it always wants to know what you can give me. Lust lusts for more sex and more money; some people lust for recognition while others lust for a change of house. The only way they could get a house was to marry someone who already had a house. That woman you are walking down the aisle with does not want you, she wants your house. That is not love; that is lust!

There you are getting all teary-eyed, thinking you found somebody that loves you. She is hugging you and all the while looking past you at your house with the two garages, fantasizing and planning on how quickly she can get the walls repainted and move her favorite furniture into your living room. The root of that scenario is not love; it is lust.

"If you ever break the cycle [of reciprocity] and stop giving you will stop the fertility of your life, and eventually, over time, you will wither."

CHAPTER SEVEN:

What Shall I Render?

Giving Back

"What shall I render unto the LORD for all his benefits toward me? I will take the cup of salvation, and call upon the name of the LORD. I will pay my vows unto the LORD now in the presence of all his people."

(Psalm 116:12-14)

What we have to understand is that when the Psalmist asks the question, "What shall I render?" he is displaying a mature mentality. A person asking that question is somebody who has come to understand that during the years when they were childish and immature, somebody had to work to put the milk in the refrigerator and turn on the lights. You know your children are growing up when they say, "Mama, what can I do to help you? What can I do to make things easier for you? I'll cut the grass, dad. Mama, you do not have to cook, I'll take care of the cooking."

"Your Harvest Without Limits"

The person who becomes concerned with what they can give is somebody who is becoming responsible. The greatest benefit of responsibility is that it opens up a door for reciprocity which creates teamwork. Unfortunately, most marriages aren't genuine teamwork, but something more akin to greed work. Working together as a team means that the first person gives what they can, you give what you can and you both become better through the partnership; each one contributing what they have toward a unified human effort. So when mature people get married they say, "What shall I render? What do you need from me? How can I make your life better?"

When the immature get married, the focus is on what they can take from their spouse. The truth is that everybody wants something back in return for their giving. Even God expects something in return. People may say they do not want anything back, but it's hard to believe that they are telling the truth. There are few people that do not appreciate being appreciated. They may not want something back in the same way they gave it to you. They may not want you to give them anything that is tangible or material, but everybody wants something back. Minimally you can appreciate someone, hug them, send them a note, or pat them on the back. Make them feel special and give something back.

Gratitude

There have been women who cooked for their families until they dropped over dead. Sadly, no one ever said, "Thank you." The inaccurate assumption was that mama just liked to cook. It does not matter how much a person likes to cook, even the best get tired of standing over a hot stove and cutting up vegetables in the middle of the night. Many things we do because they are necessary for life and not because we like to do it. People will take you for granted if they think you like to do something: "He just likes to do that. That is just the way he is. He is just strong."

You may be strong but you can use some comfort, care and even a caress every once in a while. You may think that life is somehow easy for someone else because they are wired differently than you. The truth is that it is just as hard for them to fight their way up as it is to fight your way up. The reason that they took a licking and kept on ticking is because they are survivors. Anytime there is no reciprocity in a relationship it creates frustration and bitterness. Even God expects something back in return from you. And, it is not wrong that He should ask things from you because without Him you would not exist.

The Bible says, "*In him we live, and move, and have our being...*" (Acts 17:28a). You are who you are because God allowed it. He has a right to ask things from you that nobody else could ask of you because He has given you things that nobody else has given you: life, health, strength, joy, peace, reasoning, personality, wisdom, sight, smell, touch, friends, family, resources, talents, capabilities, potential, prophecy, help, favor, status, material possessions, love, deliverance, rest and movement in your legs, feet, nose and ears.

I Am a Beneficiary

You should be deeply conscious of the fact that God has been good to you. You are a beneficiary of many things that have come from His hand. The word "beneficiary" is a unique term that dispels any myth of earning wages: you do not earn benefits, you earn wages. Whenever you are the beneficiary, you are eligible for benefits you can choose to never receive. Often you do not receive your benefits because you haven't been educated on the terms and conditions of the benefit. Sometimes you do not receive benefits because you do not know they exist. It is actually possible for someone to leave you a million dollars in their will and you not know it.

That is the reason that we attend church: so somebody can show us the will and educate us as to the terms and conditions of what is available to us. We want to know what the will says so we do not live beneath our privileges, so we dwell in peace and power, so we can receive those things that we are heir of and will not waste our life being jealous of what is in the will for others. When we realize the truth that daddy was careful to remember us then we understand that what God has for us no one can get and what God has for another, we cannot get.

Those who work at The Potter's House do not only earn a salary, they also have benefits. As full-time employees they can utilize the benefit or go to the doctor or dentist on their own and pay the bill out of their own pocket. It is the employee's choice to utilize the benefit that is available to them. If they do not have the sense to use the benefit, that is foolish. It has been provided to employees of the ministry; they can get their prescription at a reduced price, go down to the pharmacy and give them the card that says The Potter's House. It is not wages, it is benefits.

Employees are also entitled to a number of paid vacation days each year. The longer one works for the ministry, the more weeks of vacation they are eligible to take. We do not force our employees to take their vacation days. In fact, they can work the whole year without taking a vacation if they want. They are benefits, not wages, of being here at the ministry.

Not Just Stuff

When we start talking about all the benefits that God has for us, we are not talking about salvation because salvation is paid for; we are going beyond salvation. The benefit program God has for you includes things like healing, advice and direction for family, life and business. Remember the times that God healed your body? Do you recall the time God advised you; you were getting ready to do something foolish and the Lord spoke to you in the middle of the night and told you not to do it? Those are some of the benefits of having the Lord on your side. You went through a storm and God did not stop the storm, but he comforted you in the middle of the storm – that is a benefit.

We have all received some benefits in life, things we did not earn or work for. But God has been good and that is why we want to bless Him. Some of His benefits are the things He protected us from. We may have befriended people who hated us, wanted to destroy us and He protected us in our ignorance. Sometimes we were the ones trying to get to somebody who was actually trying to kill us. But God shut some doors and we are alive today. These are the benefits.

The benefits are so amazing that you can forget the pay; work for the benefits. If heaven were no more and hell was to catch on fire and burn up and there was no eternal life, it is worth it to serve the Lord for the benefits package. It is worth it all to have His benefits in this present world. He made life worth living because He was on our side and brought us through some things that we could not have gone through without Him. If He shuts down heaven and closes down hell and stops everything at the grave, we can still be glad that we are children of the King.

"The truth is everybody wants something back in return for their giving. Even God expects something in return."

CHAPTER EIGHT:

Learn to Make a Comeback

Will the Circle be Broken?

You have to learn to make a comeback. In the New Testament, Jesus helped ten lepers but only one made a comeback. Reciprocity is when something comes back to you. Ten lepers got healed but only one returned to say "thank you" to the Lord. That one leper completed the circle of reciprocity.

Your God is a circle. He is not a beginning date and end date; He is a complete circle. That is why we give a ring when we get married. It is us trying to say our love is eternal. It means the circle will not be broken and we are going to be together forever. It is supposed to make the matrimony holy. It is supposed to suggest a commitment that has no beginning or end. Despite the fact that people often break the circle, God cannot be broken. He is eternal, everlasting and unchangeable, and what God asks from you when He blesses you is that you reciprocate and give back to Him.

"Your Harvest Without Limits"

If you throw a football to someone it is a line. But when they throw it back, now we have reciprocity. If we were to draw a line following the path of the football from them to you and back, we would have a circle and not a line. We would have a circle of reciprocity. That is why when Jacob came to Bethel and he saw angels ascending and descending they were going around in a circle. God is a circle or in another word a cycle; a circle is a cycle.

Give Something Back

To get a fuller understanding of who He is you must start with the realization that God is not just a big Santa Claus in the sky giving you whatever you want. In actuality, it is only when you give back to God that you gain a full picture of who He is. He is not just God when He gives it away; He is God when it comes back. That is why He said in Malachi 1:6, *"A son honoureth his father, and a servant his master: if then I be a father, where is mine honour?"* Basically He is questioning why his children do not return good to Him. It is when you start giving back to God that you are making a come back.

Ninety percent of church folk give nothing back. They greedily line up to get everything they can acquire and then they run away. Many pastors would rather run their church on the ten percent principle. They are not concerned about the masses of people that will eat and then rise up to play, but the committed ten percent who will give back to God. These are the ones that form a circle.

Whenever somebody gives back, it increases the relationship between the two individuals. You can have seven children and love all of them. But your special attention is drawn to the child that comes back to help you in your time of need. You find you do not have to solicit their help, but they voluntarily come by to lend a hand and say, "Mama, did you need anything. Mama, are you alright. Come on, Mama, let me help you. Mama, I'll drive you."

When you are in the presence of the child that gives something back your heart skips an extra beat. We should all pray to be the kind of child that whenever the Lord sees us coming, He is glad because we are not using or abusing Him. Our heart should want to give something back to who He is and become the kind of child that He can use for anything, anytime, and anywhere.

Learn How to Fight Back

You have got to learn how to fight back. If you do not learn how to fight back, life will destroy you, devouring you from the inside out, eating you up in secret places. You will continue to walk through life like all is well: driving to work, coming home at the end of the day, still eating your breakfast putting little bananas on your cereal – all the while your insides are eating you up. Instead of being eaten up from the inside, you've got to learn how to fight back.

When you understand fighting back, that the weapons of your warfare are not carnal, you understand that a lot of things that gave you fight back in the world will not help in the spirit. In fact they are adversarial in the spirit. Simply because you were a gladiator and a warrior in the secular world does not mean you are going to be effective in the spirit because the whole technique of fighting in the spirit is different. The weapons are different, the warfare is different and the enemies are different.

In the world you were fighting what you could see. Now you are fighting what cannot be seen. Fighting things like depression and anxiety that will take over your life if you refuse to fight. Or fighting fear, where nobody knows you are afraid and you are standing up looking strong but secretly scared to death. You are fighting the fear that is waiting for you to get home tonight, threatening to jump on you; fear of failure, fear of not being good enough, fear of rejection, fear of being forsaken, being left out, incompetent, all kinds of fear.

Everything you can think of people are afraid of. But of everything you are afraid of, that depresses and discourages you and everything that would come into your life to make you bitter, you have to learn to fight back. You go against that special enemy that comes to terminate your success and destroy your future. You have got to fight back against it.

I Am Going to be Happy

Happiness is a decision. Refuse to be at this stage in life and not be happy. Decide that you are going to find a way to be happy even if you have to stop thinking about certain things and stop hanging around people who stress you out. Don't allow anything or anybody to keep you from waking up each morning and walking through the day with the happiness that you desire.

Every day is important. Don't let anyone else steal a whole

day of your life by making you miserable or upset about life. Since every day is important, count up the days and moments of bliss and peace. Take time to notice flowers, blossoms, and scents. Light scented candles because you want the room to smell good. Try to get the best out of everything and make the precious gift of today count.

You have to find a way to be happy. Enjoy watching a good comedian. If they are skilled in their craft, they can take even the most mundane events of life and make a crowd laugh. You should be glad to be able to laugh because you have had enough experiences in life to cry about.

Fix Your Situation

If you find that the circumstances in your life are unbearable, fix your situation to make it where it will be livable. If it hurts to go outside, do not go outside. If it hurts to go out the front door, climb out the window. Find a way to fight back. Refuse to be a victim the rest of your life, being depressed about events that happened years ago and mad at people who are dead and have been in the ground for decades.

Pastors live in the trash cans of people's problems. They get to see everything about everybody. Recently a pastor was talking to a lawyer and found that there was a commonality in their professions. The lawyer said that most people call him when they are in trouble, generally so much in trouble they cannot afford to lie anymore. When they are ready to go to jail for something they have done, they come clean. Pastors are able to see people from a perspective that others may never have seen them from before because people can not be phony when they get into deep crisis. The sad truth is that people do not come to you for marriage counseling until their marriage is on life support. They come ten minutes before their appointment in divorce court and stop by your office and want you to perform a miracle. For years they were fighting each other and acting like the marriage was fine and now they want the pastor to say a prayer and reverse decades of bad sowing.

Just because somebody knows how to sit in a church sanctuary, smiling and clapping and raising their hands does not mean they are not going through crisis, tragedy, or stress. If you even had a glimpse of what people were really going through, you would be ashamed of the minor events in your life that you call trouble.

"What God asks from you when He blesses you is that you reciprocate and give back to Him. When you give back, it increases the relationship between you and God."

CHAPTER NINE:

Gratitude in the Hour of Crisis

Quit Complaining

You have to come to a point and decide that you will stop complaining about your troubles because what is major to you may pale in comparison to what others are experiencing. You do not think you have a good husband, but if you only knew what that other sister was going through you would see your husband in a completely different light. Your husband may not help around the house, with the dishes or the baby, but that other woman's man may regularly beat her with a wrench.

There are people in the church that are HIV positive. They come to church each Sunday, clapping, singing, praising the Lord and counting T-cells. There are people right now taking forty and fifty pills every morning. There are people with full blown AIDS who are nicer than you. And you continue to complain how bad life is for you. You ought to rejoice and be glad in what the Lord has done for you. There are people with cancer eating up their body that are happier than you; women who have lost both of their breasts yet they are grateful for and praise God for all that He has done for them.

"Your Harvest Without Limits"

There are blind people who are happier than you and people
in wheelchairs who have a more positive outlook on life than
you. We have heard of people who have lost all of their
family, people whose house burned up in a fire and they are
the only ones who came out alive; ninety percent of their body
may be burned but they are happier than you. You ought to
be ashamed to be depressed. As good-looking, healthy,
blessed and strong as you are, as good as God has been to
you, you ought to rejoice in the God of your salvation.

The Testimony of a Dying Man

Many years ago, a couple went to see a brother dying of AIDS.
He was in the final stages of the disease and dropped from an
initial weight of approximately two-hundred pounds to a
spindly seventy-six pounds. When they entered his room he
was curled up on the bed in the fetal position. As he lay
there, they could see his bones protruding out of his body.
During their visit, they talked to him and prayed for him.
When they got ready to go the wife said, "God bless you." He
looked at her and even though he could barely talk, he said,
"He already has."

The couple staggered back to the car trying to figure out how
a seventy-six pound AIDS patient–with his bones sticking out
of his body, gone blind in both eyes, feet swollen, sores all
over his body–could lay there and say that God had already
blessed him. That visit to that dying brother changed them
forever. If that patient could be blessed only a few short days
before he died, then surely the Lord has blessed you.

Before you get depressed over your life circumstance, go and spend five days in the AIDS or burn ward. Simply look around you and see some people with real problems: people who were in car wrecks and burned; women who were burned on their hands and faces when they entered their house trying to get their baby out of the fire. Do not act as if God has not been good to you. In truth, God has been so good to you that you ought to rejoice!

Think it Over

Take some time to sit back and think of the goodness of the Lord, calculate it, adding together all the times He took care of you. You need a moment that you can rejoice in the God of your salvation. There are some people standing up to some circumstances right now that are worse than what you are dealing with. No one is saying your situation is not bad and that you do not have some real problems. No one is saying you are not upset. But be encouraged as you gain a fresh perspective on your circumstances in the light of God's goodness.

There are people dealing with crisis all around you. Some people are dealing with their problems with less money, help, talent, support and friends than you have. And, if they can make it shopping at used furniture places, wearing hand me down clothes and estranged from their family, then surely you can make it if God has blessed you with anything you need to transform your thinking about your state in life.

Transform Your Thinking

How do you transform your thinking? Paul said, "*When I was a child, I spake as a child, I understood as a child, I thought as a child..."* (I Corinthians 13:11). Thought, speech and understanding are the three factors that determine maturity. If you want to know how mature you are do not count birthdays because there are old folks that are still silly. Understanding is the truth you stand under and the truth you stand under determines your perception of yourself. Your situation does not have to change; your perception has to change.

If you want to know how mature you are, look at how you think, speak and understand. Everything about you begins in your thought life. What comes out of your mouth is the manner in which you reveal what is really going on inside you because *"...out of the abundance of the heart the mouth speaketh..."* (Matthew 12:34). If you want to know who somebody is just let them talk. If they talk long enough, they tell you who they really are.

Along with your thoughts and speech you must understand. This is the final "stand under truth" and how you can bring closure to things. I stand under this truth when I become a man and I put away childish things: thinking and understanding. All you have to do to survive life is be happy and have peace. Peace and happiness is not a husband; it is not a house, not a job or becoming prettier.
We must get rid of childish thinking, speaking and understanding. When you do that you turn into a worshipper. A worshipper worships God even in tough places. Have you ever visited a hospital where the situation was so bad that you did not even want to enter the front door, none the less walk in the room? What do you say to someone who is laying there

with a half burned body, or paralyzed from the waist down at only twenty-three years of age?

Angels Watching Over Me

It is amazing to enter the room of a person in the midst of a life threatening crisis, and instead of counseling and encouraging them, they start telling you how the Lord brought them through and strengthened them in the crisis. In the midst of a crisis someone is singing, "All night, all day, angels are watching over me my Lord." Their body might be burned and mangled, yet they are thankful that God has protected them, that they are still alive, and that His angels kept watch over their life.

Somebody somewhere is singing that song with AIDS, with cancer; somebody is singing it after their husband left them and they do not know where he is. He just walked off and left them with no help, no job, and about to be evicted from their house. Yet even in the midst of it all they still come to church for encouragement. You are sitting there with a few problem situations but somebody next to you just got a bad report. They have a lump on their breast that is hard; they are getting blood secretions on their garments. Yet somewhere in the midst of their personal crisis they are singing: "All night, all day, angels are watching over me my Lord."

"You have to come to a point and decide that you will stop complaining about your troubles because what is major to you may pale in comparison to what others are experiencing."

Section Three – A Harvest on Your Praise

"And when Jesus saw her, he called her to him, and said unto her, Woman, thou art loosed from thine infirmity. And he laid his hands on her: and immediately she was made straight, and glorified God. ...Then said he, Unto what is the kingdom of God like? and whereunto shall I resemble it? It is like a grain of mustard seed, which a man took, and cast into his garden; and it grew, and waxed a great tree; and the fowls of the air lodged in the branches of it." (Luke 13:12-13; 18-19)

CHAPTER TEN:

Influenced by Your Environment

A Great Tree

In Luke thirteen, Jesus compared the Kingdom of God to a grain of mustard seed which a man took and cast into his garden. It grew and waxed a great tree, and fowl of the air lodged in the branches of it. The same cycle of seedtime and harvest is at work here, but instead of planting the seed in the ground, the man simply cast it. The seed sprouted, grew and matured not just to fruition but to the point that it became a haven where other entities could find lodging, food, and life.

The growth of praise in the church parallels that of the mustard seed. Those of us who have been students of the Word of God for many years know that approximately twenty years ago the beginning seeds of praise teaching were sown in the Body of Christ. It was everywhere from the Catholic churches to the traditional Pentecostal churches; everybody was teaching on praise. Those were the days that we first saw praise banners and liturgical dancers in our sanctuaries. And many expositors of the Word were teaching on the different aspects and terms referring to praise.

As the years progressed, even our one-time critics and those hard-nosed, conservative churches who said they would never praise like us have started getting praise teams and praise dancers and offering 'contemporary' worship services with praise bands. Even preachers that are normally calm and quiet are getting demonstrative in their praise and coming out of their once quiet and confining shells because there is something powerful about praise.

Is Praise Magic?

A greater understanding of and practice of praise has brought many believers to a place of maturity were they have become like the mustard tree–mature enough to offer protection and ministry to multitudes. Yet, somewhere in the years of teaching and experiencing praise, we may have gotten to a place where, for many that are immature, praise is denigrated to being a tool to get what you want from God. It is vitally important to realize that we cannot teach praise as if it were magic, nor make it appear as though if you just praise God, that God is so desperate for praise, that He immediately starts handing out candy, goodies, and other blessings.

If we erroneously teach praise as if it is like magic, people will get disappointed because they praised their way out of something and then went home after church to find that their husband left them. They paid their tithe, threw a large offering on the altar, danced all the way back to their seats, and went to work the next day and got laid off from their job. When people have experiences like that they begin to wonder what in the world is going on.

For many that are young in the faith, they do not realize that praise is not some magic that you work. You cannot just enter into praise, snatch some goodies, and run off. You build up praise equity like in a house where it increases in value over time. You generally cannot buy a house today starting out with equity. Over time you build up equity and history, some pattern where you become faithful, disciplined, and consistent. God has it fixed that way because if He did not, then sinners, hypocrites, and whoremongers who come in and imitate you can get the Glory of God that you worked years to get.

Give Me Your Mantle

There was a period in ministry where everybody was asking for the pastor's mantle. Not only did they want the mantle, they wanted a double portion of his spirit and for the pastor to lay hands on them and to transfer to them the anointing that God had given him. They did not want the trouble that the pastor went through, the burdens that he bore; they did not want to endure the gossip or the controversies. No, they wanted the benefits, but they did not want any of the attack that went along with the blessing of the Lord.

They wanted prosperity and they wanted the healing, but they did not want to endure the gossip and the ridicule, the contradictions and the adversity, the sickness, pain and struggles. They did not understand that all of that builds up the equity that eventually releases the blessings of God on one's life. You cannot enlist in the army as a general. You have to work your way up through the ranks and go through some processing.

What happens is that when the Word of God is going out in a church service, inadvertently some principles are taught and some others are caught. You diligently write notes and you get some of them, yet some of them come from associations where you just catch them. It was not so much that Naomi was a teacher or that she was prophetic, it was her mannerisms that affected Ruth. Ruth simply caught the faith of Naomi.

Have you ever just caught something? No one taught it to you, but by being in the presence of another, their mindset somehow fell on you. You do not even know the moment when it came on you, but all of a sudden you started reacting differently because you had been influenced by your environment.

The Transformation

If that principle can work positively in someone's life, it can also work negatively. If you take a young boy and put him in a maximum security prison at age sixteen, after spending a period of time with inmates who are hardened criminals he will evolve and become like those he associates with. It does not matter if he did not come from that background, he just catches that background.

In the same way that happens in the positive if you are put around seasoned Christians who love the Lord, who manage their emotions, who do not have temper tantrums, who aren't flipping out and cursing people out, who aren't living double lives, some seed will fall on you and you will catch it.

Altar call is a wonderful vehicle for change but sometimes the greatest change in a life often occurs when the people are still sitting in their seats. If nothing happened to you while you were sitting in the seat, coming to the altar will not fix you. Conviction, change, and revelation have to hit you in your seat. All of a sudden while the Word is being preached, you just catch something. It may be something you heard before, but all of a sudden it sounds different today than it did any other day.

That is why you need to be in the house of the Lord, particularly when there is a move of God in progress. Go to a church where you can become a part of a move of God. Not simply religious rhetoric, but you need to be there because you never know when you are going to catch something that is going to give you a breakthrough in an area that you have been dealing with for years. Sometimes you have to come to church even when nothing is going on because you have to build up equity.

The Diversion

Jesus mentioned His encounter with this woman in Luke 13 taking place during a season of ministry. This woman was really a diversion from Jesus' teaching ministry. Jesus was up teaching and He saw her in the crowd, bowed over and bent out of shape. The Bible says that she had carried her infirmity for eighteen years and when Jesus saw her. He called her and told the woman, *"Thou art loosed from thine infirmities."* The Bible says that He laid His hands on her and immediately she straightened herself up and began to glorify God.

Following her obvious healing a conversation broke out where the people began to challenge the rulers of the synagogue and Jesus about healing this woman because it was the Sabbath day. Technically the rulers said that He had no business working on the Sabbath. The Lord rebuked His adversaries that had spoken up and this woman continued to praise God.

Jesus returned to teaching and it was then that He said that the kingdom of heaven was likened unto a man who cast a mustard seed out into his field. What Jesus was doing was explaining the process of planting the seed, that there is a time element; you do not plant a seed and reap a harvest immediately. Jesus was bringing focus on the fact that there is a time mechanism for the seed in that it needs time to grow.

> *"It is vitally important to realize that we cannot teach praise as if it were magic, nor make it appear as though if you just praise God, that God is so desperate for praise, that He immediately starts handing out candy, goodies, and other blessings."*

CHAPTER ELEVEN:

Testing the Seed

The Placebo

The idea that it will take time for your seed to grow may not make you shout and it might get on your nerves, but ultimately sooner or later—whether you do it kicking or screaming, whether you do it here at church or in a jail cell, or whether you have to go away and join the army—everything living has to grow up. If you do not have a disease, dysfunction or mental retardation, ultimately you have to grow up. There are some people who do it more quickly or slowly than others; there are some people that fight it down to the end, but eventually it is unavoidable; if you stay alive you have to grow up. You might be physically big, but you have not grown up. I have seen people who are big on the outside but small on the inside because they have not grown up.

Just because you look grown up on the outside does not mean you are grown up on the inside. By the same token, just because you look, shout, and dance like a seasoned Christian, does not mean that you are a seasoned Christian. When a pharmaceutical company is testing a new drug, they have the actual medicine and they have a placebo. You cannot outwardly tell the difference between the medicine and the placebo. They do this intentionally so there will not be any psychological inducement affecting the outcome of the results. If you are helping with the test, you do not know what you are taking because the placebo looks like the real thing.

In the church we have real praisers and we have some who are placebos. Outwardly they look the same, shout, dance and sing the same, but one of them is a fake, coated over with an outer façade of praise, while the other one has been through hell and high water and tested in the furnace of affliction. If you cannot tell the real deal from the false outwardly how can you tell which is real and which is fake? To do so you have to break it open and get into the inside and test it. If you do not go through the test you cannot prove that you are the real thing and not a placebo.

Take the Test

It is the test that determines whether you are authentic or if you are imitating the real deal. If you are not tested you can tell me that you are the real deal, but when you go through a test the truth comes out. If you are sowing or throwing seeds out in the garden and in the midst of the real seeds, I have some fake seeds, you can soon tell the real from the fake because the fake seed is not going to grow. If you are still falling out about the same things that bothered you years ago, you should be suspicious because you are still living the same way you were years ago. If you are still moody and hateful, be suspicious because if you are the real deal there should be a change in your life, heart, and attitude.

Even if you want to be changed you may go through the process kicking and screaming. If you are honest you will admit that God made you grow up. He did not let you act like a fool; He whipped your back side, straightened you out, and developed your character; you had to grow up. Jesus progressed from healing this woman—a controversial healing that brought on attack and criticism—to talking about growing a mustard tree.

"The kingdom of heaven is like unto a man who cast a mustard seed out into the garden and it grew up and became a tree." What Jesus is teaching is that we are in a process that is going to take some time. A pastor was in South Africa a few years ago following the end of apartheid and delivered a message to people living in the poor, racially segregated townships, encouraging the people to hold on to God. His premise was that their condition did not go wrong in one generation and it would not be straightened out in one generation. Every generation will continue to get stronger because coming out of something is a process.

There is a Process

We do not want to hear anything about process because we want everything to be instantaneous. Our culture has trained us to want everything immediately. We want everything now— a three minute egg and grits in sixty seconds. And for the benefit of those that did not grow up in that era, there is a difference between quick grits and the slow-cooked type processed over time. You think you have it down pat but there is a difference between Duncan Hines pound cake mix and taking a pound of butter and two cups of sugar, whipping it up and beating in an egg one after the other.

There is something to be said about the process and taking the slow road, taking time, and developing. It may take longer, it may be inconvenient and dirty up more dishes, but when it is all over the quality the process produces is so much greater. Jesus was indicating that they criticized this woman because of one day, but what happened to her that day did not start that day. The process of praise does not begin the day you get the breakthrough. The process of praise begins when you get no breakthrough at all; it begins with eighteen years of coming to church like that woman, looking like everybody else was being blessed but you. But you have a spirit that says, "*Though he slay me, yet will I trust in him…*" (Job 13:15).

Raising children is a process, not instant grits. You do not just throw in some Scriptures, send them to school and pop, here comes a perfect child. It is a process that includes problems, headaches, and struggles. But if you stick to it, what you put in them will eventually come back out. Being a great preacher is a process. You cannot get there quick. You can be exciting and make a name for yourself quickly, but that has nothing to do with being a great preacher. A great preacher is somebody whose ministry affects the lives of people and causes them to be changed and not just excited.

When Praise Does Not Work

When the Lord took the children of Israel to the Promised Land it was not so much about them getting to the destination as it was about them going through the process. He could have brought Israel through a shorter and quicker route, but they would have missed the advantage of the things they needed to learn in the process. There is something that we all learn through the process, when the tears are streaming down our face and we cannot feel any joy, and the presence of the Lord seems far away.

This is not about when praise works, but when praise does not seem to work and you are bowed over, sick and afflicted and everybody else appears to be doing better than you, but you are still seeking God. Some think that the woman started praising God when she got healed, but that is not true. The eighteen years of her faithfully coming to church in her broken condition—that was praise.

When you see someone, they are praise. When they show up in the house of God, it is as praise to God. It was not praise that got the woman healed; it was the eighteen years of diligent, relentless, radical, "I am coming regardless if anyone helps me" attitude.

Process Before Promotion

The process in our life always comes before the promotion. The greater the process one walks through, the greater the promotion will be. "*For unto whomsoever much is given, of him shall be much required...*" (Luke 12:48). Before God can promote you, He has to process you. You can't give up on

your promotion. You praised Him broke, you praised Him
sick, you praised Him depressed, confused and frustrated.
You were discontented and you still praised God. You cried
yourself to sleep and still went to church to worship the Lord.
You have been through hell and you are still here praising
God.

The devil tried to make you pull back from trusting God for
the harvest in your life. He attempted to put a wedge between
you and God in your thought process, but you told him that
you would never let him separate you from your God. You
have been through hell but you are still here marking time.
Some days it may seem like you do not see any progress, but
you are still here. Often, circumstances appear to be getting
worse, but you are still here. Continue to worship and praise
God all the way until the day that your harvest is ready to be
reaped.

*"It is the test that determines whether you are
authentic or if you are imitating the real deal.
If you are not tested you can tell me that you
are the real deal, but it is when you go through
a test that the truth comes out."*

CHAPTER TWELVE:

The Transformation

The Power of Passive Praise

Most of the individuals who were healed in the Bible were healed because they were aggressive. They were assertive people who cried out, screamed, and crawled through crowds so they could touch the hem of Jesus' garment. Contrary to the assertive norm, the woman in Luke thirteen said nothing. As Luke narrates the story, the woman had a totally passive attitude as she sat back and said, "I am in your presence. It is up to you. I know you are able, you do not have to heal me and yet I will still believe you are able. If it is my lot in life to come in here like this, if it takes me longer to do things that others do quickly, I am still going to put one foot in front of the other, get in my position and sit."

Job's wife told Job, "Why do you not '*curse God and die*' (Job 2:9). Go ahead and end your life because you do not like the process," and he said, "I am going to stay right here and praise the Lord because '*…he knows the way that I take.*' (Job

23:10)." In other words, God knows where you are. The same God that knew where Job was knows where you are. God knows what is going on in your house, your family and your financial situation. God knows the stress and duress you are under right now. You do not have to scream or shout to get His attention. Simply rest in His presence and the knowledge that He is able to *"...do exceeding abundantly above all that we ask or think, according to the power that worketh in us..."* (Ephesians 3:20).

Look How Far You Have Come

For those of you experiencing the growth test in your life have you considered that you are probably going through something right now that would have driven you crazy only ten years prior? If you have learned to be nice to people who you would have once cursed, if you have learned to help somebody who you know lied on you and treated you badly, you know that Jesus is working in your life. It could be none other but Jesus Christ growing in you, influencing a positive change in your actions and reactions to your family, friends and co-workers.

Thank the Lord now for the years of nothingness where He developed and tested your character. Be grateful for the years when you had nothing to do but study. Give God thanks for teaching you to endure gossip, ridicule and backbiting on the backside of the desert before putting you in the spotlight. If He would have put you out front before the world any sooner it would have killed you.

What God is about to give you will be so powerful in kingdom influence that if you do not go through the process you will not be able to stand up under its weight. You see, if you do not learn to be faithful over a few things, how can you be given much?

Your Defining Moment

Do you wonder if that woman in Luke thirteen knew that the Sunday she went to church was going to be the tipping point in her life? It was that particular day that a new Rabbi was coming to minister; she did not know much about him, but decided she was going to church no matter who was preaching. Think about all the factors that could have influenced her to stay home: the preacher was a new guy with no reputation, it would take her a long time to get there, and once she arrived there would be no handicap parking spaces or elevators to make a sickly woman feel more comfortable. Nothing about the scenario was convenient but she came on out there anyway.

While Jesus was up preaching he saw her. She did not have to do anything for her praise to work. She did not have to slap anybody and she did not have to scream out. He saw her after her eighteen years of suffering and said to her that it was her day. Can you believe that everything you went through throughout your whole life is preparing you for one defining moment? Can you believe the situations that you were praying about, that you thought were real problems, were just preparation for one defining moment? Every task, pain and every burden was building up to one moment where everything would change.

Out of everybody in the room Jesus decided He was going to use her. Why? The reason is that she was not a placebo. She was not somebody who was serving Jesus for the fish and loaves. She was not just there for a quick blessing and she was not there saying, "If you give me a job, I'll praise you." Her attitude was that without a job, with no healing, sick in her body, she was still there; she was with Him all the way. Jesus says, "Today, I am getting ready to change your season."

"Everything you have gone through is preparing you for one defining moment; one moment where everything will change."

CHAPTER THIRTEEN:

The Turnaround

Something Good is About to Happen

You have probably learned that when something good is about
to happen, when God is about to deliver you from a situation
that you have learned to live with, it is usually preceded by
you getting to the place where you stop murmuring,
complaining and fussing about the problem. God wants to
bring a turnaround in your life, a complete one-hundred-
eighty-degree transformation, a transition into another
dimension of harvest. A key to that happening is that you turn
your complaints into praise.

Through years of tears and adapting to the trials and
difficulties of life, you must come to the point where you
make up your mind if He does not change the circumstances
in your life, you are still going to praise Him. What you will
find is when you get to that place, He will then move in your
life because you have matured enough to realize that God is
worthy regardless of all the things He does for you. It is at

that point that God can move in your situation because you have grown up and stopped complaining.

Some of you reading this book have been building up power and gathering equity while you have been down in the trenches, locked up in obscurity, being overlooked, ignored and ostracized. Some of you are about to explode; something great is about to happen in your life. You learned some character skills, you passed some tests, endured hardness and you did it without a complaint rolling off your tongue. You have suffered long and now you have a feeling in your belly that you are on the verge of something that will rock the world as you have known it. You do not have the words to explain to anybody what it is that is taking place, but you know that God is about to do something great.

You ARE Loosed!

For the woman in Luke thirteen, the moment of her healing built up in her for eighteen years. There is somebody reading this book that God has been preparing and it has been building in you for multiple years. Jesus calls the woman to the forefront and He speaks to her. He does not say, "Woman, my word to you today is that I am ready to loose you; or, woman, you could be loosed today." Jesus said, "Woman, thou art loosed" not 'will be loosed,' not 'was loosed,' but 'thou art loosed.'" The word loosed is in the past tense. In other words, the woman was coming into what Jesus had started to do in her eighteen years prior.

Jesus was communicating to her that she had finally grown
into a dimension that He could give her what He planted in
her eighteen years before. When the word that she was
loosed hit her, she was struck with the realization that all of
the fears and anxieties that had been her companions were
lies. The truth of the matter was that Jesus was bigger than
the thing that was holding her. All of her circumstances were
lying about who she really was. She realized that as a King's
Kid she could stop the lying voices whenever she got ready.
The Bible says that immediately she straightened herself.

That is one of the main reasons that you need to attend
church, to get the Word so you can understand who you are,
so that you can rebuke every lying spirit that is stopping you
from coming into the blessings of God, and so that you can
straighten up. You can get out of this yourself. You need to
believe the Word that says, "...*with his stripes we are healed*,"
(Isaiah 53:5), the Word that says, "*Blessed shalt thou be in the
city, and blessed shalt thou be in the field*," (Deuteronomy
28:3) and the Word that says, "*And the LORD shall make thee
the head, and not the tail; and thou shalt be above only, and
thou shalt not be beneath*" (Deuteronomy 28:13).

You Are an Overcomer

The Word of God says that you are an overcomer even when
your circumstances say you are broke, cursed, sick or old.
Whatever your circumstance consists of, it is telling you what
you cannot be. But know right now all of your circumstances
are lying on you. 'Immediately' is how quick you are going to
come out of a condition that has been going on for years in
your life. In the name of Jesus, it is not going to take you

eighteen years to get out. Immediately, straightway, suddenly, quickly, God is going to snatch you out of it.

The Luke thirteen woman was healed so quickly that the devil could not do anything about it. By the time hell got the message that she was healed she was already walking around praising God. While she was praising God a lynch mob of lying spirits arrived on the scene. Since the devil could not stop her healing, they attempted to derail her blessing by getting her to stop praising God. When your focus shifts from praising God to responding to your critics you will lose your blessing. You need to be smart enough to keep on praising God while they are talking about you.

This woman had been handicapped for so long she was used to being different. She was used to being looked at funny and having people make fun of her. Everything she had gone through for eighteen years had taught her how to deal with this moment. She never opened her mouth to them but she kept praising God. You need to shut your mind to all criticism and give God a crazy praise. Tell the devil, "It is over, I am coming out; it is too late, the scales have tipped. Rivers of living waters are flowing out of my belly, I will bless the Lord at all times!"

God Will Deal With Your Enemies

There's another reason why you should not say anything to your enemies. What you need to do is keep praising God because while the woman was praising God the Lord was dealing with the enemy. Praise is much more than thanksgiving; it is a weapon of warfare and when you start praising, God will deal with your enemies. If you are going to fight your enemies, God does not need to fight them for you. But if you will be still, you will see the Lord fight your battles.

You're probably thinking it does not make sense that those people were arguing about that woman's right to be healed. It was too late because she was already healed. The Lord said that that was precisely the point. He said that the problem with His people is they think they are having problems because they do not have the breakthrough. The reality is that you are having problems because you *do* have the breakthrough. If you were not in the center of God's will the enemy would not be as angry as he is. Instead of trying to get the enemy to shut up, you should rejoice in what your Daddy has given you.

"But Lord", you may ask, "If she was already healed why did the enemy send those adversaries?" He said, "To distract her from what I was doing in her life." The battle was not to get healing because she was already healed. The battle was to not get distracted. Your enemies do not have any power over your blessing because you are already blessed. Your enemies are simply trying to tempt you to be distracted. If this woman had stopped dancing and started arguing she would have forfeited her blessing. Fortunately, she knew that she was a daughter of Abraham, a King's Kid, and continued to praise Him for the good thing He had done in her body.

"Praise is a weapon of warfare and when you start praising God, He will give you the breakthrough."

Chapter Fourteen:

I Shall Come Forth

Mature Praise

This woman, after eighteen years of training, had matured to the point where she was disciplined enough to maintain her focus in the face of criticism. And though others talked about her, they could not take from her what God had done in her life. This leads you to a major point. The Bible said that her critics were His adversaries. Did you know that your enemies have become His enemies? Did you know that the battle is not yours, it belongs to God? Did you know all you have to do is keep on praising God?

The Bible said that when the people saw her praising God, her being attacked, and Jesus rebuking her enemies then the *Joy* that was on her fell on them. God is going to use what you are going through as a witness to people around you. When they see the dignity with which you go through your trouble, then the joy that is in you is going to fall on them, your home, and everything connected to you.

That is why the Bible says that when the mustard seed grew up it became a tree and all types of fowl were able to lodge in its branches. It is the same for you. As you have grown in your understanding and worship of God, you have created a tree of mature praise that has become a place for your family and friends to find shelter. When you stop praising God based only on paychecks and water bills, who loves you, who called you or did not call, and you reach a point of consistency in your praise then God is going to draw out all of the treasure that is shut down in your life.

Come Forth as Pure Gold

Praise is more than action, it is attitude. People can imitate your actions but they cannot fake your attitude. All of the placebo people who are after your position, your husband and your job, they can imitate your actions, but not your attitude. What seals the deal on your praise is not just your action, but it is the attitude of praise. It is more than saying, "I thank you," it is being thankful. It is much deeper than praise; it is an attitude of worship that says no matter what season I am in I am still thankful.

Job said, *"…he knoweth the way that I take: when he hath tried me, I shall come forth as gold."* (Job 23:10). In modern English this means that the Lord knows where you are and when this test is over you will come through it purified. You can have the assurance that whether you are dealing with your job, family, marriage, ministry, finances or health that God knows where you are. And when this season of life is over you are going to come out of this smelling like a rose. That is why whatever state you are in be content because when this is over you will come forth as pure gold.

In Luke chapter thirteen, Jesus had opened the Word to
minister, paused and said, "Wait a minute. I will not speak a
sermon; I will make this woman a living sermon." Did you
ever consider that God is making you a sermon and the best
sermons always end on a high note? The sermon of your life
may have sub-points that deal with trial and crisis, but the
final summation of the message is that through it all you will
come forth.

It is Not You They Want

It is very easy when you are going through something to
misunderstand it. You are being fought and attacked and
you're trying to understand the reasons why. "What in the
world is going on?" you ask. "Why are they fighting me? Are
they trying to shut me down, trying to stop me from getting to
the place that God has for me?" Have you ever felt on the
verge of a breakthrough and it seems that some fresh enemies
were sent your way to fight you?

The Lord is faithful to answer your questions. He says they are
not fighting you over where you are going, but they are
fighting you because they are angry about where you are. He
then reminds you that He has always used your enemies to
announce to you where you are. It is their attack that makes
you realize where you are.

In this passage of Luke, the people weren't really interested in
fighting the woman; they did not care anything about that
woman. They were only using her to fight her leader.
Her attack was not even about her, it was about her
leadership. When you became yoked to a ministry that is

moving internationally, affecting the lives of countless thousands, whether you want to or not you connect with the attack against that ministry. And if you do not tangibly connect with the vision of that ministry, you are being attacked for something that you do not understand. The good news is, *"No weapon that is formed against thee shall prosper; and every tongue that shall rise against thee in judgment thou shalt condemn"* (Isaiah 54:17). You will come forth as pure gold if you keep your praise.

"You will come *forth* as pure gold if you *keep* your praise."

Section Four – The Harvests of the Wheat and Tares

"He answered and said unto them, He that soweth the good seed is the Son of man; The field is the world; the good seed are the children of the kingdom; but the tares are the children of the wicked one; The enemy that sowed them is the devil; the harvest is the end of the world; and the reapers are the angels. As therefore the tares are gathered and burned in the fire; so shall it be in the end of this world. The Son of man shall send forth his angels, and they shall gather out of his kingdom all things that offend, and them which do iniquity; And shall cast them into a furnace of fire: there shall be wailing and gnashing of teeth. Then shall the righteous shine forth as the sun in the kingdom of their Father. Who hath ears to hear, let him hear." (Matthew 13:37-43)

CHAPTER FIFTEEN:
The Incorruptible Seed

Born Again

"Seeing ye have purified your souls in obeying the truth through the Spirit unto unfeigned love of the brethren, see that ye love one another with a pure heart fervently: Being born again, not of corruptible seed, but of incorruptible, by the word of God, which liveth and abideth for ever."
(I Peter 1:22, 23)

You were born again by the Word of God, not of a corruptible seed but an incorruptible seed. Despite the clarity of this passage in Peter, there are many misconceptions in the world today about the meaning of salvation. Many of these misconceptions are promoted by the religious systems of men. Salvation is not just joining the church. Salvation is not rosary beads, crosses and candles, catechisms, church creeds or doctrine manuals. Salvation is the gospel of the harvest in its truest form—when the Word of God pricks you in your unbelieving heart and convinces you that the thing missing in your life is Jesus.

That seed germinates down in your soul and you are born again by the incorruptible seed which is the Word of God. It can happen in church or in your car. It can happen in the middle of the night and it can even happen in a smoke-filled nightclub, sitting on a bar stool with a glass of your favorite alcoholic beverage in your hand. God does not care where you are when He invades, what He cares about is that He finds faith in your heart. You could spin around on that bar stool and say, "I am sick of this, something is missing in my life," and before you hit the exit door, eternal life can invade your soul; that is salvation.

What is amazing is that the same seed that gets down into a good woman will impregnate a whore. You do not have to be a nice, neat little person on your way to the Salvation Army to hand out blankets to the homeless for God to save you. You can have a needle hanging out of your arm and years of cocaine use has burned all the hair out of your nose. But if the Word of God pricks your heart it will bring about eternal life down in your spirit. You can smell like a marijuana factory, but if God invades your spirit, His seed is so powerful and so potent that conception will happen right there. You are born again by the Word of God.

Pricked in Their Hearts

"*Then Peter said unto them, Repent, and be baptized every one of you in the name of Jesus Christ for the remission of sins, and ye shall receive the gift of the Holy Ghost.*"
(Acts 2:38)

Most Christians are so familiar with Acts 2:38 that you can wake them up out of a coma and they could quote it. The verse has been emblazoned on buttons, pens, and on bumper stickers on the back of our cars. But even though we are familiar with verse 38, we do not take the time to look back a verse at Acts 2:37 where Peter was preaching on the day of Pentecost. When those listening heard his preaching, the Scripture records that "*…they were pricked in their hearts.*"

When the Bible says that they heard Peter's preaching and 'they were pricked in their hearts' it means that the Word of God had penetrated their heart. "*Now when they heard this, they were pricked in their heart, and said unto Peter and to the rest of the apostles, Men and brethren, what shall we do?*" (Acts 2:37).

There are two main things happening to these people in this one verse: one is 'faith,' which is them being 'pricked in their hearts' and the second is 'works,' which is them asking, 'what shall we do?' The Bible says that, "*Even so faith, if it hath not works, is dead, being alone*" (James 2:17). When they were pricked in their hearts it means that Peter preached something that penetrated that hard fleshly hymen around their hearts. When he pricked it he left a seed, which is the Word of God, in their heart.

Conception

When the Word of God enters the womb of your heart, the egg of your faith attaches to the Word and conception occurs. Once that happens nobody has to beg you to be converted, baptized or live holy. If your faith is real, your works will prove it and you too will say 'what shall we do?' People who have been pricked in their hearts by the Word of God are gentle, receptive and open to the Word of God.

Some of the folks in the church today are difficult because they are in the building but not in the kingdom. The sad reality is that many of the people in the church have never had a legitimate experience with God's Word. That is why they cannot obey, follow instruction, will not submit, do not tithe, do not give, and will not serve or work; their hearts have remained unbroken.

If a person's heart has remained unbroken, they are a virgin to the Word of God. A virgin can be around men, but merely being around men does not impregnate them. You can be around the church, but being around the church does not make you born again. "*Marvel not that I said unto thee, Ye must be born again*" (John 3:7).

"God does not care where you are when He invades your heart, what He cares about is that He finds faith in your heart."

CHAPTER SIXTEEN:

The Gospel of the Harvest

THE WHEAT AND THE TARES

"Another parable put he forth unto them, saying, The kingdom of heaven is likened unto a man which sowed good seed in his field: But while men slept, his enemy came and sowed tares among the wheat, and went his way. But when the blade was sprung up, and brought forth fruit, then appeared the tares also. So the servants of the householder came and said unto him, Sir, didst not thou sow good seed in thy field? from whence then hath it tares? He said unto them, An enemy hath done this. The servants said unto him, Wilt thou then that we go and gather them up? But he said, Nay; lest while ye gather up the tares, ye root up also the wheat with them. Let both grow together until the harvest: and in the time of harvest I will say to the reapers, Gather ye together first the tares, and bind them in bundles to burn them: but gather the wheat into my barn."

(Matthew 13:24-30)

"Your Harvest Without Limits"

There is a dynamic in this parable: the wheat and the tare are both growing up together at the same time in the same place. Jesus takes the next few verses and teaches on this subject explaining that this is what the kingdom is like. In the kingdom, you are going to have both the wicked children and the righteous children growing up together. And both the wicked and righteous are prospering because growth is the equivalent of prosperity. In the parable, it is not like the children of the kingdom are growing up and the wicked are dwarfed. The Bible says that in the morning they both sprang up together.

Later in Matthew 13:37-43, Jesus vividly explains the kingdom parable of the wheat and tares growing up together. For many of the other parables that we read in the Bible we are left to teach and explain their content without the benefit of Jesus sharing how he would exegete the text. This parable is one exception to that rule, as the interpretation of this text is not left up to the discretion of the preacher or author. Jesus personally explains the meaning of this particular parable because he wants to be sure we do not miss the real meaning. This is the gospel of the harvest. It works in your body, business and faith; this gospel works in every area of your life.

Growing up Together

There is a dichotomous situation that we have in today's world. In this country we are building stronger ministries than we have ever built in our national history, making full use of the airwaves, internet, television and movies. We are using all the resources and technology available to break into new dimensions for the gospel than we have ever used before. We are finding new and creative avenues to package and promote the timelessness of the message of the cross and salvation, so that everyone living in our time and sphere of influence will have the opportunity to hear about Jesus.

But, while we are expanding the Kingdom of God through all avenues, the same Internet that is streaming the gospel is streaming pornography. The same screens that are showing the *"Passion of the Christ," "Woman, Thou Art Loosed,"* and *"Left Behind"* are also showing movies consisting of every imaginable degrading, ungodly story line. They are like the wheat and the tares, all growing up together.

And if we consider the situation of iniquity abounding in our world, the Bible says that *"where sin abounded, grace did much more abound"* (Romans 5:20). Both iniquity and grace, the wicked and the just, evil and godliness are growing up together and engaged in a fight against each other for the souls of men and women. They are fighting each other for the same airwaves, television space, finances and allegiance of the masses of humanity on this planet.

Fighting for the Same Soil

Recently a journalist published an article complaining about people giving finances to the church. His premise was that the churches are bilking poor people out of their money. Unfortunately in some cases this may be true, but for every crooked clergy, there are a multitude of churches and ministries doing great things and supporting great causes. The fact that there are people abusing the system does not mean that there is something wrong with the system; it means that there is something wrong with the abusers.

The second point in addressing the journalist's premise is why he was outraged about poor people giving money into the kingdom, but he said nothing about the lottery. Where are lengthy articles about the money being hoarded in great big lotteries where poor people are spending their pay checks on a chance to get lucky? Why did the journalist not write about the casinos and their owners and put pictures of the owners' houses and the cars they drive in the paper? And why didn't they show how people are going into the casinos on binges, spending their rent and retirement money at the roulette wheel and slot machines?

If the journalists' real concern was about protecting poor people from being bilked and mistreated, let's shut down the lotteries, close down the casinos and the money-grubbing preachers and we can all go to the altar together. The problem is that the world promotes the lotteries and casinos with full-page ads in the paper because like a tare growing up with the wheat, that is okay. On the contrary, anything that strengthens the kingdom calls for an outraged cry. The reality is that the wheat and the tares are fighting for the same ground because neither of them can grow without being planted in a certain type of soil.

"Both iniquity and grace, the wicked and the just, evil and godliness are growing up together and engaged in a fight against each other for the souls of men and women."

CHAPTER SEVENTEEN:

The Harvest is Past

Have We Missed the Harvest?

Jeremiah 8:20 presents a principle that is important for us to understand. It says, "*The harvest is past, the summer is ended, and we are not saved.*" That may be one of the most condemning, frightening statements in the Bible. The basic meaning of the passage is that there is a time when you will simply run out of time—run out of time for making excuses and for walking in your foolishness and mediocrity—all the things that you have allowed in your life that have kept you void of an understanding of the things of God.

There is going to come a time in your life and in history that the harvest will be past, the summer ended and yet we are not saved. Jeremiah goes on to say, "*For the hurt of the daughter of my people am I hurt; I am black; astonishment hath taken hold on me. Is there no balm in Gilead; is there no physician there? why then is not the health of the daughter of my people recovered?*" (Jeremiah 8:21-22). The Lord said that He has enough balm – an ointment, a healing influence – so that you do not need to remain hurt the rest of your life.

There is a balm in Gilead! You can recover if you want to. You can become all that God has destined for you to become in the kingdom, but you are using your affliction as an excuse. And you are foolish because you do not realize that you are running out of time.   The harvest is past. The crop has already been brought in and there is nothing more in the fields remaining for you to reap. The summer is ended; the season for reaping is past and no amount of desire or change of heart on your part can make it not be so. And still, we are not saved!

Excuses

Could it be that you are wasting time making excuses, using dysfunctions as a cop out not to develop yourself into the man or woman that God wants you to be? Could it be that you are so busy trying to harvest some money, a career, a future and all varieties of consumable material goods that are going to perish with you, that you have not harvested the most valuable thing that you could ever harvest in your life, which is your soul and eternal life?

Could it be that you have majored in the minor and minored in the major? Could it be that you have given your best strength to raising up hordes of corruptible things and given your lesser strength to the things that pertain to life and godliness in Christ Jesus? If you take a moment to look out on the field of your life have you fertilized your tare and starved your wheat to death so that all you see is the tares outgrowing your wheat.

And now the harvest in your life is about to pass and the summer is about to end and does it even matter to you about being saved? Many people are wondering if church folk are even concerned about being saved. People are more worried about cutting five minutes off the time they spend getting out of the parking lot and have no interest in or excitement about the broken people seeking God at the altar.

A Passion for the Harvest

There was a time in the church when ten people coming to the Lord would have provoked a celebration. Today, hundreds of souls come to the altar, yet people walk past like it is ordinary. If the church has lost her passion about salvation, then what of the world? If salvation means nothing to us, it means absolutely less than nothing to the world and life goes on with business as usual. Unfortunately, while we are doing business as usual, the harvest is passing and the summer is ending and multitudes are still not saved.

Jeremiah 9:1 says, "*Oh that my head were waters, and mine eyes a fountain of tears, that I might weep day and night for the slain of the daughter of my people!*" The question is "Where has the weeping gone? Where are the people that are glad to be saved?" In the absence of real anointing, we substitute what really draws people to Christ with blessing plans and bus ministries, camping trips and spiritual lotteries. We draw people in with the boast that we have the best choir, the best technology, and we have an orchestra. We did not previously need an orchestra to get people to come to Jesus. In times past there was a fervent, infectious and intoxicating prayer around the altar and the saints would hit the streets and bring people to Jesus. They would brag about how many people they won to the Lord, not how many Rolls Royce's they owned. Today the church is becoming worldlier and the world is becoming churchier. They do not call their talk show hosts, 'Pastor,' but they are pastoring the people and although they are getting spiritual they are not offering salvation.

The prayer requests from a short ten years ago are vastly different from the prayer requests that we get now. Years ago, prayer requests included a long list of names from people desiring their children and grandchildren to obtain salvation before they died. Today, prayer is more along the lines of: "Stand with me that God will bless me to open a business in three months. Pray that I can get an extra house in Tahiti or intercede for me that I can get my hair done without using my credit card."

Malnourished by Inaction

"In the mean while his disciples prayed him, saying, Master, eat. But he said unto them, I have meat to eat that ye know not of." (John 4:31-32)

In the interaction here between Jesus and the disciples, the disciples were so carnally minded that all they were worried about was getting something to eat. On the contrary, Jesus was so filled with purpose that he said he had meat to eat that they knew nothing of. In other words, Jesus is communicating that He was nourished by doing the will of God.

Some of you are suffering from malnutrition. You do a real good job of going to church, but you do a poor job of *doing* the Word of God. You like to sit in the pew and hear the Word as long as the preacher does not preach too long. Although you may chew or nibble on the Word in church, you are fooling yourself because you only receive nourishment when you activate what you are being taught and start participating in the Word of God.

Jesus said, *"...I have meat to eat that ye know not of. Therefore said the disciples one to another, Hath any man brought him ought to eat? Jesus saith unto them, My meat is to do the will of him that sent me, and to finish his work. Say not ye, There are yet four months, and then cometh harvest? behold, I say unto you, Lift up your eyes, and look on the fields; for they are white already to harvest."*
(John 4:32-35)

God did not put you on your job only for the money you receive in your bi-monthly paycheck. The truth be told, your company did not hire you for you to get rich; they hired you to help them get rich. Jesus has a higher purpose for you on that job; he put you there to meet another stream of people that you can influence by the way you live, think and function. But because you are not cognizant that you are running out of time you have overlooked the fields that are already white to harvest.

There is a misconception in the church today that what we call church growth is in reality great preaching. Great preaching is not church growth. Great preaching is feeding the people that the saints harvested. The pastor is not supposed to preach people into the church. The congregation is supposed to bring people in while the pastor feeds them once they come. In the absence of true soul winners in the church, we now have to sing and preach them in because nobody is going out to get them. The unfortunate result of this phenomenon is that church growth has become something more like a shifting of the saints or stealing sheep.

LABORERS IN THE HARVEST

"...behold, I say unto you, Lift up your eyes, and look on the fields; for they are white already to harvest. And he that reapeth receiveth wages, and gathereth fruit unto life eternal: that both he that soweth and he that reapeth may rejoice together. And herein is that saying true, One soweth, and another reapeth. I sent you to reap that whereon ye bestowed no labour: other men laboured, and ye are entered into their labours." (John 4:35-38)

In the city of Dallas the shifting of saints is quite obvious. All one has to is subtract the smaller number of local persons who attend church from the vastly larger number of the population of the Dallas metroplex to see that only a small percent of the population is even being reached for the Lord. There are millions of people in Dallas driving down the highways, sitting in the clubs and shooting up in the alleys: lost souls without a relationship to the Living God. The sad reality is that because the church has gotten lazy, we have to hold on to who we have in the pew because we have no plans to go out and save anybody else.

In the John four passage Jesus elaborates for us the role of the laborers in the process of sowing and reaping. He also tells us that the time of the harvest is now. Since Jesus said that two thousand years ago, how long do you think harvest time is going to last? How in the world can we act like we still have four months until the harvest? Could it be that we are coming to the end of the harvest and the summer is past and still we are not saved?

"Jesus has a high purpose for you. He placed you in a stream of people to influence by the way you live, think and function."

CHAPTER EIGHTEEN:

The Second Harvest

The Thief in the Night

In the seventies, one of the main topics that preachers were preaching was the soon coming of the Lord, and that the believer had to be prepared because Jesus would return like a thief in the night. Believers, constantly looked over their shoulder and up in the air, especially whenever they did wrong. They were driven by fear that He would step down and snatch the worthy saints, and leave others behind.

Eventually saved ones began to think, "How could He come like a thief in the night and surprise everyone when every preacher was preaching about it, talking about it and looking out for His arrival?" Little did we know that in a few years nobody would be saying anything about it, want to hear about, or talk about it. And if He came today it is not the world that would be shocked, the church would be shocked. The church has become so carnally minded that He would have to pull us loose from this place as we spout our objections to His

timing: "I have a promotion coming up; we are moving into
our new house next week; I just bought a field and yoke of
oxen; I have to bury someone; do not come now!"

The Ingathering of the Harvest

We seem to have lost all concepts concerning seedtime and
harvest. The day of Pentecost in Acts chapter two is the
celebration of the ingathering of the harvest. When Pentecost
comes into our life, it pushes us into full-time harvest.
Through Pentecost in our lives God is empowering us to
gather in the harvest. Could we be running out of time? Are
our children saved? Does it matter any more? Are our youth
ministries saved? Are you saved?

When Jesus speaks about the gathering of the harvest He is
actually referring to two harvests. The first harvest is what we
are currently experiencing where people are being preached
to through TV, books, tapes and live presentations, and are
hopefully pricked in their hearts and make a decision to
follow Christ. As believers we have an active part to play in
the gathering of this first harvest.

And, certainly, we can do a better job of gathering in the
harvest. It begins in our house and it breaks out among all the
people with whom we have influence. God puts each of us in
different circles and gives us favor with different audiences so
we can infiltrate their environment and affect them positively.
But for many in today's church, we are busy becoming like the
ones we should influence. In a strange reversal of kingdom
principle, the church is actively studying how we can be like
the world, instead of how we can affect them.

The Second Harvest

There is going to be a second harvest. Revelation 14:13 says, *"And I heard a voice from heaven saying unto me, Write, Blessed are the dead which die in the Lord from henceforth: Yea, saith the Spirit, that they may rest from their labours; and their works do follow them."* When real saints die they go on to rest in the presence of the Lord, but, while they can rest from their labor, they cannot be rewarded.

They cannot be rewarded because what they taught and what they did is still being perpetuated in the lives of other people. Multitudes of people are still using the revelations, teachings and tools that they created. To be absent in the body is to be present with the Lord (2 Corinthians 5:8). That moment, while they are beating on your chest attempting to jump start your dead heart, you are present with the Lord. They would be shocking the shell that you lived in while all the good stuff had been pulled out of the shell to be present with the Lord.

Most pastors could not be paid for their ministry. If they ever said anything that blessed you, or that you quote or use as you go out and minister the Word, they are still getting dividends on their ministry. Blessed are the dead that die in the Lord for their works will follow them. Your works will follow you and will come in for generations.

THE HARVEST OF THE EARTH

"And I looked, and behold a white cloud, and upon the cloud one sat like unto the Son of man, having on his head a golden

*crown, and in his hand a sharp sickle. And another angel
came out of the temple, crying with a loud voice to him that
sat on the cloud, Thrust in thy sickle, and reap: for the time is
come for thee to reap; for the harvest of the earth is ripe."*
(Revelation 14:14-15)

The harvest of the earth is not the harvest of the gospel. The
harvest of the earth is the harvest of the tare. The children of
the wicked one are becoming riper. Look around you at how
many things are permissible now that were unthinkable a mere
ten years ago. We are actually debating about same sex
marriage. Matrimony is a theological term generally
accompanied with the word 'holy,' but matrimony has become
so secularized that it has now become a matter of how it is
interpreted constitutionally not theologically.

And we are having a serious argument. Not about people
who are struggling in their sexuality, needing prayer in their
attempt to recover. We are having an argument about
legitimizing something from which we need healing. What
does that mean? It means the earth is getting ripe.

Hatred of ministers and ministries has increased. Today, you
can be respected for doing anything but being a preacher.
You can get on a talk show and claim you hear messages from
the dead and our culture will respect you and put it on the top
notch shows in this country as a religious option. You can lay
out in a yoga position and say, "I am one with the earth and
the elements," and it is perfectly acceptable; you are
respected. You can be anything you want to be, but when you
say that you are a Christian, you have to be broke, poor and

quiet. What is this all about? The harvest of the earth is ripe.

Have you ever wondered why in your lifetime you have gone from watching *Mayberry* to watching *Queer as Folk?* Have you wondered why in many cities it is easier to get a permit for a strip joint then it is to get a permit to build a church. Why have spirits of divorce infiltrated the world, climbed into the church and now the odds are against you having a successful relationship? Why are many of the people writing manuals about marriage making millions of dollars teaching you how to be relational when they have been married three or four times? The reason is that the harvest of the earth is ripe.

THRUST IN THY SICKLE

And Jesus is saying, *"...Thrust in thy sickle, and reap: for the time is come for thee to reap; for the harvest of the earth is ripe. And he that sat on the cloud thrust in his sickle on the earth; and the earth was reaped"* (Revelation 14:15-16). There are going to be two harvests: the harvest of the wheat which is what we are engaged in now and the harvest of the tare which is what Jesus called the children of the wicked one. They each will be harvested into different places. One will be gathered into bundles to be burned. One will be gathered into heaven and eternal life.

Which harvest do you want to be in? There is an angel with a sharp sickle who is waiting on a command from God who will say, "Since they missed this harvest, thrust thy sickle into the earth because the earth is ripe." The earth is ripening while you are reading this book. Miss it if you want to; there is another one coming that is not optional. Jeremiah, the prophet said, *"I see a time that the harvest is past, and the summer is ended, and still we are not saved"* (Jeremiah 8:20).

Still week after week, Sunday after Sunday, opportunity after opportunity, still we are not saved. If altar calls are done effectively, people would come from everywhere to be saved. Heed the warning of the second harvest so that you can respond to this harvest, accept the Lord in your life and be saved.

"When Pentecost comes into your life, it pushes you into full-time harvest. Through Pentecost, God is empowering you to gather in the harvest."

102

CONCLUSION

Where are you in the cycle of seedtime and harvest? Are you saved? If you have never opened up your life to receive Jesus as your Lord and Savior, we invite you to do so now. Pray this prayer:

> *Lord Jesus, I confess that you are the Son of God who died for me, and shed your blood to cleanse me from all sin. I acknowledge that I have been living a life that is not pleasing to you. I am sorry for my rebellion and for ignoring you and your Word. Forgive me for all my sin, wash my heart and conscience clean with your precious blood. Fill me with the power of your Holy Spirit so that I can understand the Bible, learn how to pray and grow in my relationship with you, and live my life in a way pleasing to you. I thank you Jesus for saving me and including me in the harvest of the wheat!*

If you sincerely prayed that prayer, the next step is to begin to spend some daily time reading your Bible and praying. Also, find a local church where you can be taught the Word and experience fellowship with other believers.

If you were already a believer when you opened this book, take the principles you have learned and apply them in your daily life. God is going to do something wonderful for you; the harvest to come will be greater than anything you could imagine or think: a harvest without limits.

Diligently do whatever is necessary to prepare to become a successful reaper: sow good seed, pull out weeds, learn to reciprocate, praise through all circumstances, and let God take you through the process of developing maturity in you. Be assured that once you have been tested, you too shall come forth as pure gold!